BLACK SEPARATISM: a bibliography

BLACK SEPARATISM: a bibliography

Betty Lanier Jenkins & Susan Phillis

under the auspices of

Metropolitan Applied Research Center, Inc.

Greenwood Press

WESTPORT, CONNECTICUT • LONDON, ENGLAND

Library of Congress Cataloging in Publication Data

Jenkins, Betty.
    The Black separatism controversy.

    1. Black nationalism--United States--Bibliography. I. Phillis, Susan,
joint author. II. Metropolitan Applied Research Center. III. Title.

Z1361.N39J45 [E185.615] 016.30145'19'6073
ISBN 0-8371-8378-2   75-23866

Library of Congress Catalog Card Number: 75-23866
ISBN: 0-8371-8378-2

First published in 1976

Greenwood Press, a division of Williamhouse-Regency Inc.
51 Riverside Avenue, Westport, Connecticut 06880

Printed in the United States of America

Cover design by Mike Fender

contents

Preface   **ix**

Introduction   **xiii**

Part One: The Separatism vs. Integration Controversy

1. HISTORICAL PERSPECTIVES   3

   The Beginnings   1760–1864.   3

   Reconstruction and After   1865–1953.   8

2. THE TWENTY YEARS SINCE <u>BROWN</u>   17

Part Two: Institutional and Psychological Dimensions

3. IDENTITY: INDIVIDUAL AND COLLECTIVE   42

4. EDUCATION: SEGREGATION AND DESEGREGATION. . .   59

   Elementary and Secondary Schools   59

   Higher Education   71

5. POLITICS: COALITIONS AND ALTERNATIVES   95

6. THE ECONOMIC ORDER: BLACK ENTERPRISE,
   BLACK WORKERS AND INCOME   109

7. RELIGION AND RACE: CHURCH STRUCTURES
   AND REDRESSING INEQUITIES   118

NAME INDEX   128

TITLE INDEX   145

To my Mother
and to the memory
of my Father

B. L. J.

preface

It was the resurgence of separatism in the public statements and behavior of many blacks, especially of students and young adults in the late 1960s, that led to interest in a review of the literature having to do with black separatism in the United States. In 1969 a group of scholars was first brought together by the Metropolitan Applied Research Center on the campus of Haverford College to discuss the changing role of the Negro intellectual. At subsequent meetings of this group—which came to be known as the Hastie Group, MARC was asked to compile a bibliography documenting the antecedents and current status of the black separatism controversy. * Much of the impetus for this request came from concern about the controversial and bitter manifestations of separatism among black youths on college and university campuses.

The acute and sometimes dramatic responses of separatism that surfaced in the 1960s were not new to the experience of blacks and whites in the United States. Separatist behavior, attitudes and ideology have been practically coterminous with the presence of blacks in America. Blacks formed their own churches and mutual benefit societies in the late eighteenth and nineteenth centuries in protest against segregation and discrimination. In 1815 Paul Cuffee organized a colonization project to take Negro settlers to Sierra Leone. The first Negro newspaper was established in the 1820s. From the 1830s through 1850s the Negro Convention Movement flourished and provided the means for debate among Negro leaders as to whether to take separate, all-Negro collective action or to accept whites as participants in their drive for equality. Reconstruction brought an upsurge of support for emigration and colonization projects with such prominent persons as Alexander Crummell, Henry Highland Garnet and Martin R. Delany playing important public roles. The Black Zionism of Marcus Garvey's Universal Negro Improvement Association attracted a substantial number of followers after World War I; and important residuals of the Garvey brand of nationalism have persisted and been given new respectability since the late 1960s.

Separatism may be seen as a contrast conception and stance with economic, political and cultural dimensions. In general, it has waxed and waned as the conditions and hopes of blacks in the United States have fluctuated. In the recent past, high expectations for significant improvement in status and continuing serious commitment to equality in the United States have withered. Disillusionment and disappointment were expressed not only in the violence and destruction of Watts, Newark, Detroit and other communities but also in the resurgence of nationalist-separatist sentiments of various hues.

---

*See Kenneth B. Clark's essay for a listing of the members of the Hastie Group, p. xiii.

This bibliography does not attempt an exhaustive or complete examination of the literature pertaining to black separatism. The aim is to present historical as well as contemporary writings and to include various kinds of writings—scholarly, journalistic, protest and polemical.

The bibliography consists of two major sections: Part One, "The Separatism-Integration Controversy" and Part Two, "Institutional and Psychological Dimensions." Part One is divided into two chapters on "Historical Perspectives" and "The Twenty Years Since Brown." Part Two is organized functionally rather than historically—the major parts: "Identity: Individual and Collective," "Education: Segregation and Desegregation," "Politics: Coalitions and Alternatives," "The Economic Order: Black Enterprise, Black Workers and Income," and "Religion and Race: Church Structures and Redressing Inequities."

Within each chapter, selections are listed in alphabetical order by author's last name or by title. The annotations provide a brief summary of the substance of the works. Citations followed by an asterisk are annotated in another chapter and can be located by looking up the title in the index. Selections are included in a chapter on a particular historical period not only if they were published during that period but also if they were written about the period later. Name and title indexes are provided. Unpublished items such as letters, speeches and papers are deposited in the MARC Library.

We acknowledge with appreciation the sponsorship of the Metropolitan Applied Research Center and the support of the Hastie Group as well as the constant encouragement and sensitive criticism of Kenneth B. Clark and Hylan Lewis; the editorial assistance of Mary S. Strong and Jeannette Hopkins, and the contributions, at various stages of preparing the manuscript, of Adrienne Faison and Richard M. Newman.

May 1975

Betty Lanier Jenkins
Susan Phillis

One ever feel his two-ness—an American, a Negro; two souls, two thoughts, two unreconciled strivings; two warring ideals in one dark body, whose dogged strength alone keeps it from being torn asunder.

The history of the American Negro is the history of this strife,—this longing to attain self-conscious manhood, to merge his double self into a better and truer self. In this merging he wishes neither of the older selves to be lost. He does not wish to Africanize America, for America has too much to teach the world and Africa. He does not wish to bleach his Negro blood in a flood of white Americanism, for he believes . . . that Negro blood has yet a message for the world. He simply wishes to make it possible for a man to be both a Negro and an American without being cursed and spit upon.

W. E. B. DuBois
August 1897

introduction

Kenneth B. Clark
Ralph Ellison
Adelaide Cromwell Gulliver
William H. Hastie
Hylan Lewis
J. Saunders Redding
Bernard C. Watson
Robert C. Weaver

Some Personal Observations on Black Separatism

KENNETH B. CLARK: Six years ago MARC invited a small group of Negro writers, social scientists and public officials—Kenneth B. Clark, Mamie Phipps Clark, St. Clair Drake, Ralph Ellison, John Hope Franklin, Adelaide Cromwell Gulliver, William H. Hastie, M. Carl Holman, Hylan Lewis, J. Saunders Redding, Anne Cooke Reid, Robert C. Weaver, Eddie N. Williams and Franklin H. Williams—to meet at Haverford College and discuss the precipitous rise of black separatist thought and activity among Negro college students. The individuals who assembled at Haverford were chosen because they knew each other in other settings and shared the conviction that racial integration was essential to racial progress and justice in America. Bernard Gifford and Bernard C. Watson joined the group in 1972.

These individuals also had no delusions about the problems and the difficulties inherent in seeking racial justice in America. They did not expect that the historic Brown decision of 1954 would function as a magic wand and immediately eliminate all past vestiges of racial cruelty and oppression and leave in its place an interracial Garden of Eden. There would be continuing struggles. There would remain the past consequences of legally and institutionally reinforced segregation. But what had previously not been clearly understood in the first stages of optimism following the Brown decision and in the excitement of racial confrontations of the early 1960s was that the rigid walls of racial segregation had left very deep anxieties in many Negroes concerning their ability to compete in the larger society on a single standard of achievement.

The clamor of a minority of articulate black students at interracial colleges for racially separate residential, social and, in some cases, academic facilities on white campuses must be seen as an expression of racial insecurities resulting from past segregation. This epidemic of separatist demands on the part of organized groups of black students can be interpreted as symptomatic of the psychological stresses caused by the new challenges and threats of a nonsegregated situation. That many of these young people sought to explain their separatist ideology and demands under the guise of "racial militance" merely betrayed their poignant and pathetic racial fears.

Five or six years ago it was a common experience of black scholars who were invited to speak at such colleges as Oberlin, Swarthmore, Cornell, Columbia, Yale, Princeton or Harvard to be challenged by black students for harboring "archaic" integrationist views. In many cases these students refused to participate in any discussion of social issues unless they could exclude white students. Their heroes were only those blacks who shared their black racist anxieties and fears. Only those black scholars who agreed with the students' demands for separate black studies programs, separate black social facilities and cultural centers were applauded. Black scholars who dared to question the logic, the strategy and morality of black separatism were at best ignored and at times sharply challenged, cursed and sometimes threatened.

This pattern of ideological, rhetorical and functional racial separatism was reinforced by the ease with which white administrators made rapid concessions to the separatist demands of their black students, by the mindless support of these demands for separate black programs and facilities by some black leaders and some "liberal" whites as well as by the disproportionate and uncritical coverage of student demonstrations by the media.

During this period of intense and much publicized separatist activity on the campuses, the vast majority of the folk Negro did not themselves become advocates of black separatism. According to surveys of opinion among Negroes, no more than 15 per cent of a representative sample of Negroes ever expressed any sustained rejection of the goals of racial integration. Nor did they accept black separatism as an effective approach to racial justice in America.

This general lack of support in the black population indicated that it would be just a matter of time before the wave of black separatist activity and ideology would begin to recede. One dared to hope that eventually black students would become suspicious of how readily white college administrators granted their requests for separate facilities. It should have been obvious that the almost obscene haste with which these racially segregated facilities and courses were established under the guise of racial progress was quite consistent with residual racism.

It is difficult to determine an exact point at which black students began to question their own role in the reinforcement of racism on the college campuses. Did the emotionalism and verbal fads and postures just lose their attention-getting appeal? Were the hard realities of the average black's continued struggle for justice and dignity sufficient to break through the academic isolation and pretenses of their children? Whatever the reasons, these black students eventually began to examine their own motives for demanding that they be segregated. They started by acknowledging that their desire for separate facilities reflected personal and collective insecurities, fear of rejection and, more specifically, the fear of competing with whites who were more privileged economically and academically.

Once these fears and anxieties were expressed and no longer totally obscured by the rhetoric of militance and assertions of race pride, it became possible to talk more rationally about what the real and most difficult racial challenges were. It could then be seen that solid bases for pride could only be found in specific personal achievement based on a single standard of intellectual, academic, social and moral qualities. It was then possible to understand that security could not come through racial isolation and that in a modern world one must be prepared to communicate with and to interact with others who differ in such superficial characteristics as color, religion, nationality or culture. Racial isolation on college campuses could not and did not in reality increase one's personal and group security. And certainly black students did not need to leave the confines and constrictions of their ghetto communities in order to be racially isolated on a college campus. Finding security through the challenge of higher education was much more complex and demanding.

Once the militant rhetoric, the emotional name calling, the threats, the bombast and the coercion subsided, it was possible to begin serious discussions with some of these students. One could then ask them to reflect upon and examine the meaning of the challenges, the risks and the sacrifices made by their parents and their grandparents in the historic struggle against American racial cruelties and segregation. One could ask what would have been the consequences if their parents had tried to rationalize the acceptance of racial segregation—and tried to pretend that it had some intrinsic virtue instead of being imposed upon them.

The most obvious consequence of such earlier racial retreats would be that these students themselves would not be at interracial colleges—placing themselves in the absurd position of asking for racially separate facilities. With the beginning of serious communication, some of these students began to understand that there is no easy road to the elimination of racial cruelty and oppression. For each step of progress there had to be individuals who had the courage to fight for their acceptance as total human beings. Racial progress always depended upon the fact that there were some individuals with the courage to refuse to accept arbitrary exclusions and with the will to fight against all the flagrant and subtle forms of the superstition of racism—whether these were initiated by whites or blacks.

This was the perspective—indeed, the conviction—of what has come to be known as the Hastie Group which first met at Haverford in 1969. The members of this group took seriously the important responsibility of articulating the rationale and the goals of racial integration in America. They accepted this responsibility in the face of the threats and riducule and rejection from their own young people. They expressed their values and beliefs without apology. They refused to be intimidated or coerced. They refused to imitate the demagogues in seeking momentary popularity and applause. Each member of the Hastie Group in his own way—in writing and in speeches—stated what he or she considered essential for the continued struggle for racial justice in America.

They showed no failure of nerve—and the suggestion for the preparation of this bibliography is symbolic of their concern for contributing to the strengthening of the present and future generations of Negro students.

Seven members of the Hastie Group—Ralph Ellison, Adelaide Cromwell Gulliver, William H. Hastie, Hylan Lewis, J. Saunders Redding, Bernard C. Watson and Robert C. Weaver speak to the issue of separatism in the short introductory essays that follow.

* * *

RALPH ELLISON: In spite of all the writing I do, and for all of the
lectures I give each year, there are many matters which I don't write
about; nor, except with my wife and a few intimate friends, do I discuss
them. Perhaps this is because they have to do with ideas, emotions
and attitudes which grow out of my situation as a Negro American and
with those undefined and uncodified aspects of our lives which require
the sympathy and insight usually found only among those who have been
conditioned and disciplined by our specific group experience. Today
such in-group discussion is no mere luxury; it is a necessity both for
ourselves, for our restless youth and for the American intellectual
community as a whole. There is no question but that my own participation in our discussions at Haverford had something of the effect of a
catharsis. I was cleansed of some of my doubts and confusions and,
thankfully, I was stimulated—not by the sound of my own all too famil-
iar voice, but by your ideas and by your passion. If this is to any extent true of the other participants I believe our enterprise was well
worth the effort and should be continued on a permanent basis. Certainly it points to the necessity of our no longer working in isolation
from one another, and it is clear that we have much to offer that has
been missing from discussions in the larger American intellectual community. There is simply no avoiding the fact that there are many aspects of American life which can only be described, analyzed and defined by black intellectuals, for no other group possesses an adequate
perspective or so urgent a need.

In summing up what I tried to say in our discussions I would emphasize my personal affirmation of integration without the surrender of
our unique identity as a people to be a viable and indeed inescapable
goal for black Americans. As a writer who tries to reduce the flux and
flow of life to meaningful artistic forms I am stuck with integration, because the very process of the imagination as it goes about bringing together a multiplicity of scenes, images, characters and emotions and
reducing them to significance is nothing if not integrative. Further,
the object of my fictional imagination is the American society and the
American experience as experienced fundamentally by Negroes and I
find it impossible to deal with either in isolation, for they are intri-
cately united in their diversity. The judgments implied by the fictional
products of my imagination might well repudiate many accepted American values and definitions of reality, but this by no means infers that
the integrative role of the imagination (and of the intellect) is invalid.
It does imply that the larger American ideals of freedom are the ultimate ground upon which any literary evaluation of the cost, pain, joy
and triumph of being human is tested.

The American people is united in all its regional, class, ethnic
and religious diversity by a bond of language. There are many idioms
of that language and it is partially the creation of a voice which found
its origin in Africa. Indeed, it began to be influenced by that voice
long before the American nation was formed. In the beginning was the
word and our voice sounded in the language with which the word was
spoken. The American language owes something of its directness,

its flexibility, its music, its imagery, mythology and folklore to the Negro presence; it is not, therefore, a product of "white" culture as against "black" culture, rather it is the product of cultural integration. And the realities of discrimination and racism notwithstanding, it is a fact that culturally the melting-pot has indeed melted and that one of the strongest forces shaping the general American culture has been what I call the Negro-American idiom.

I am calling attention to the cultural pluralism of American life because until the present college generation that pluralism as expressed in the art, folkways and style was an important source of Negro American optimism—just as that optimism was a support of the general faith in the workability of the American system. Our elders recognized their presence and influence in areas of American life from which they were physically barred, and while the American house was of many mansions they knew that despite racial discrimination there was something of themselves dwelling in most of them and not merely as servants. Sometimes they made hue and cry over the theft of their substance and their style, and sometimes they were silent but they saw themselves in all the movements of American life no matter how confused the scene. For them the problem was not that of identifying with the scene but of having others give public recognition of their contribution. Certainly there was no question of trying to withdraw in a pique and of surrendering their investment in the experiment.

Today that sense of having shared creatively in the common American experiment is under an assault by passionate young blacks who have lost their mooring in tradition. They are romantic, earnest and ignorant, a state for which I believe that we as intellectuals are responsible because in pursuing our specialties we have failed to interpret the past and define the present and project the future in ways that are available to the young. Far too frequently black youth has been forced to depend upon intellectuals of other groups for interpretations of their relationship to the larger society. In fact other groups of intellectuals have given more time to the task than we ourselves. Often they appear so obsessively concerned with defining our life styles, character, traditions and values as to reduce us to silence and pliable inaction. Frequently they seem motivated by a desire to manipulate our image for political and economic purposes of their own, and some have taken the concepts of Negro sociologists and turned them against us, creating thereby much confusion and great resentment. But whatever their motives, there is the fact that they are functioning as intellectuals, and it is their legitimate task, as it is ours, to explore the wholeness of American life and the interrelationships between the various groups which compose it.

That they have co-opted our role is a criticism of ourselves, for we have failed to address ourselves effectively to many of the broader problems of American life, and we have failed to follow up our often creative analysis of specifically Negro American problems into the broader areas where they inevitably lead. In other words, we often forget that the only way to be an effective Negro intellectual is by being

a most perceptive and responsible <u>American</u> intellectual. I believe that
the state of black youth point to our failure and if we have failed them,
then we have failed American youth generally. For all their talk of
black separatism—really another version of secessionism, an old American illusion which arises whenever groups reach an explosive point of
frustration—and for all their stance of alienation, they are really acting
out a state of despair. They are frightened by the existence of opportunities for competing with their white peers on a basis of equality which
did not exist for us. They suffer traumatically from the shock of sudden opportunity. The shackles have been struck from at least one of
their ankles and the skin is sensitive to the turbulent air and the illusory
possibility of absolutely unrestrained movement. Actually they are in
the position of pioneers who must enter an unknown territory armed
only with the knowledge and skills which they've brought with them from
the past, but instead of plunging in and testing themselves against the
unknown, they choose rather to argue with the deficiencies of the past
and to direct accusations against their parents. They accuse us of
lacking manhood and courage and they have declared themselves a new
breed, which perhaps they are. One thing is certain, they have thrown
us a challenge and I believe that we should meet them head on. I don't
think that we should be put in the position of apologizing for our back-
grounds, values or goals but I do think that we must provide a forum
wherein the unwritten wisdom of the group can be intellectualized and
passed on to those who are sincerely seeking for answers and orientation.

* * *

ADELAIDE CROMWELL GULLIVER: Perhaps the most important consequence of the Haverford meeting and Ellison's evaluation of it is the
focus placed on the role and responsibility of the black intellectual. For
too many years and to too many people, the black intellectual has truly
been "the invisible man or woman" of our race. Circumstances of control over our institutions by whites and the resulting need for radical
change have eliminated from our communities—or certainly from positions of influence—persons dedicated to the pursuit of truth and knowledge. However, they have not eliminated persons dedicated to either
political strategy and popular rhetoric or research programs designed
merely to attract government or foundation funding.
    Along with the gains of the 1960s—black youth in employment,
racial pride and greater access to education—must be placed the critical loss of the visibility of the black intellectual and the legitimacy of
an intellectual tradition among blacks. I have been amazed to observe
that young adult blacks are almost as ignorant as whites not only of our
historical roots but of the complexity of our present communities. In
some simplistic way they see only super-blacks, bourgeoisie and
themselves as constituting the people. If intellectuals are ever identified, and usually they are not, they are coupled with the bourgeoisie

and characterized accordingly. This ignorance stems from many sources: the lack of impact and voice of black intellectuals, white influences (the white world also easily overlooks us) and the break in continuity between the generations in the black community. For all their separateness and proclaimed uniqueness, the young blacks of the sixties imbibed from their white peers many values, not the least of which was a culture of youth which saw no relevance in age, in experience, or in knowledge.

This ahistorical and anti-intellectual posture of the young blacks led them inevitably to a dead end. Yet as with most social trends, the seeds of decline were being sown at the height of its emphasis. And the significance of the Haverford meeting was that a small group of black intellectuals—in spite of the climate of the time—was trying to address the problem of their invisibility and ineffectiveness. For these intellectuals well knew that they were the legatees of a noble tradition among blacks and that if nothing else were true, they knew where the water holes were as well as the immense size of the desert.

A public declaration today of our concern at the time of our greatest rejection by the younger blacks could possibly provide a sound basis for rebuilding our ties, of exerting an influence now when only the most uninformed, ill-trained or recalcitrant black cannot see that black Americans are and must be a part of this society; that there is no retreat; no hiding place on this planet; that riots and rhetoric may have a function but are not solutions; and that as black people and citizens of this country, we are going to stay here, having a full share of whatever there is, giving to it according to our abilities and that we have the potential and strength to achieve these goals.

* * *

WILLIAM H. HASTIE: In 1950, addressing a predominantly black audience on a college commencement occasion, I had this to say about integration as a goal toward which we should be and were moving in American race relations:

> We have not been pleased by our isolation from the mainstream of American culture. But many of us have become accustomed to it. This is one of the evil consequences, perhaps the worst, of a long-endured caste system. When old restrictions of caste are relaxed, it is hard for the oppressed to throw off the ways of thinking and acting that their oppression has inculcated.

Then I added:

> We have concentrated our attention upon what government and the general community must do to eliminate racial barriers. We have pointed to the

> the road that white America must travel to join us in
> a democratic society. But that road is a two-way
> street. From one end it begins in the ghetto, the
> mental as well as physical ghetto in which we have
> lived so long. We must move out of that ghetto,
> throwing off its influence as we go, so that we ar-
> rive at a meeting point genuinely free of the self-
> defeating habits and attitudes that our long servitude
> has taught us.

Reading these 1950 observations twenty-five years later, I am convinced not only that they were valid then but also that their validity is even clearer today. Certainly, the number of black and white Americans who relate to each other as individuals without racial hostility, tension or reticence has increased manyfold since 1950.

This is not to say that the psychological consequences of long-continued racial isolation and subordination have disappeared from the American scene. Unfortunately, some of the otherwise praiseworthy militance of blacks during the 1960s was disfigured by race hatred and by the exaltation of supposed virtues of racial isolation and willful withdrawal from the mainstream of American life.

But the separatist wave may well have crested. The 1970s seems to be a time of greater awareness that in our society ethnic isolation is stultifying and counter-productive. Yet on that issue we are still far from consensus. For this reason, the wealth of material identified and catalogued in this annotated bibliography should help those who are interested in and perhaps puzzled by the ideological disagreement between integrationists and racial separatists to reach their own rational conclusions.

* * *

HYLAN LEWIS: As I mused about black separatism and its personal meaning to me—a black male adult who was born a colored infant before World War I, spent all of youth and most of adulthood as a Negro, and became black for public purposes of identification a few years ago through no initiative of my own, I thought about a political homily uttered less than ten years ago by Stokely Carmichael, "Every Negro is a potential black man."* I immediately turned it on its head, noting that it

---

*The fact that mention of Carmichael's name is likely to trigger for adults the question, Whatever happened to Stokely? and for many youth the puzzled query, Who is (was) Stokely Carmichael? is an especially wry commentary on the fleetness of fame for the person whose cry, "Black power!" in Mississippi in the late 1960s was to reverberate so mightily for a rather brief period. And it is also a reminder that changes have taken place in the meaning of black in a fraction of the time necessary to assess the situations of blacks.

is also true that "every black man is a potential Negro." Carmichael's comment about the black potential in every Negro was at once good social analysis, a twist on DuBois' classical mirror metaphor, as well as a shrewd political gambit. It bespeaks these American truisms: every Negro/black person has a large repertory of responses to racial discrimination and powerlessness; and "separatism" and "integration" are variable companion themes that have marked, and will continue to mark for the foreseeable future, the responses of black/Negroes to the persistent, entrenched racism (institutional and other) of American society.

The political and the psychological salience of separatism and of integration is constantly changing, and sometimes it changes very rapidly. It should be noted that such changes occur independently of what blacks call themselves or are called in the United States. Historically, whether one called oneself or was called colored, Negro, black or Afro-American had no necessary bearing on whether one perceived oneself or was perceived separatist or integrationist, militant or nonmilitant. Always marked by some invidiousness, black and Negro recently became acutely politicized for a rather brief period as one result of the civil rights crisis; and at the same time separatist and integrationist became umbrella labels, having more to do with the politics of race among blacks than with the politics of race between blacks and whites.

Once the separatist themes and styles of argument were revived, politicized, and in many instances, exploited cynically by blacks and whites, acute ruptures of meaning between blacks and blacks as well as between blacks and whites appeared. These ruptures of meaning were not, and are not, over what blacks should call themselves; at root, they were and are in many ways over whether blacks should concede the United States to whites—partially or wholly, temporarily or for good. The grammar and the rhetoric of the new separatism—the differing rationales, logics, procedures and time schedules for conceding the field or parts of it and for regrouping—have made for fragmentation, diffusion and diversion. Confusion has resulted from attempts to make separatism which is essentially a loose political label and not a program, synonymous with pride, militance and the necessary path to racial equality. Separatism represents voluntary racial disengagement; at best it is perceived and rationalized as a temporary, strategic disengagement. In practice, it is a design to give positive affect to selected withdrawal behaviors and dispositions in the black community; it is, in fact, the most episodic, sad and despairing of gestures in response to the ways in which whites use political and economic power and derive benefit from the exclusion and disadvantage of black Americans.

The more one thinks and talks about the dynamics and the consequences of separatism in the United States, including a fresh review and assessment of the rapid changes of recent times, the more one gets reinforcement for the firm view that separatism would be undesirable as a condition voluntarily accepted and intolerable as a status imposed. One also becomes convinced anew that, short of genocide or mass suicide, separatism is impossible for American blacks in any meaningful and enduring sense.

* * *

J. SAUNDERS REDDING: The only final solution to the problem of race is that of forming a single societal community with full membership for all. Resistance to this will be strong. A multiracial democratic society jeopardizes its existence when any one of its component groups enjoys only partial democracy. This is not to say that ethnic as well as religious and cultural pluralism should not continue and cannot make positive contributions to the "inclusive American community." But identity in this respect need not and should not imply discrimination. Inclusion must not be qualified by any of the factors that have hitherto made for exclusion and perverted the spirit of what I hope growing numbers of Americans believe they are or want to be.

And, finally—black Americans are American. In spite of the Black Muslims and the ambivalent appeal of their emotional identification with Muslim Africa, the black American is no more African than the fairest Anglo-Saxon Protestant is. He is American. To quote Kenneth Clark, "His destiny is one with the destiny of America. His culture is the culture of Americans, and so are his vices and virtues, and so are his problems."

* * *

BERNARD C. WATSON: Racial integration is a crusade in which most black Americans have participated in one form or another. The common enemy was clearly perceived as segregation of the races enforced either by law or common practice. The costs of such enforced segregation were all too clear: unequal opportunity in every area of the nation's economic, political and social life. Enforced segregation had and continues to have as its ultimate result a denial of full participation for all citizens in a genuinely pluralistic society.

But the struggle for a truly integrated pluralistic society has been long, bitter and fraught with unanticipated consequences. The costs have been high: economic and physical oppression, repression of human optimism, and outright dehumanization.

What appeared to be major steps forward led to new difficulties. The Brown decision of 1954 is illustrative. When the U.S. Supreme Court declared separate schools inherently unequal, many assumed that the millenium was just over the horizon. Within a few short years, however, thousands of black educators were dismissed, demoted or assigned out of their areas of competence; many black institutions were closed, all in the name of integration. Thousands of black students were suspended, expelled, physically brutalized or psychologically assaulted. Massive resistance to desegregation was attended by

intimidation, violence and even murder. Many black Americans won-
dered: Is the goal worth the costs?

Concurrent with the Civil Rights Movement which led to significant
gains—public accommodations, voting rights, provisions for non-
discrimination in certain areas of employment and promotion—was the
development of new pride in our unique identity as black Americans, as
a people. Again, however, an unanticipated consequence for some
black Americans was a retreat, a turning inward toward our blackness
with a consequent rejection of cultural integration, even of cultural
pluralism. For some, the decision to reject cultural pluralism was
rooted in philosophical orientations; for others the wellsprings were
bitterness and fatigue after a long struggle resulting in what some perceived to be limited gains. For still others, the rejection was the result of ignorance, a lack of knowledge, internalizing rhetoric without
understanding its substance or its meaning. Whatever the source, the
phenomenon became known as black separatism.

To this black American, it appears obvious that a withdrawal or a
retreat—partial or complete—from the struggle for equality and full
participation in all aspects of the society is a denial of our history.
Black Americans have been fighting for options and full participation
for more than 300 years. Every aspect—political, economic, cultural—
of this society has been enriched by the brains, sweat and blood of black
Americans. It is as much our country as it is the favored groups', and
we are entitled to all the rights, privileges and options available to the
most favored of its citizens. To continue to struggle for integration in
a pluralistic society without sacrificing, compromising or losing our
unique identity as a people is a difficult, but worthy and necessary un-
dertaking.

To learn, to relearn, to continue to deal with overt and covert
racism may be depressing, frustrating and difficult in the extreme.
But it is an essential part of the continuing educational experience for
all minority peoples, especially blacks. For our youth it must be an
essential part of their educational experiences. If our youths are to
deal effectively with whites in later life, as they must, they might as
well begin on the campuses. They cannot do so by retreating to the illusory havens promised by separate courses of study, dormitories or
other exclusive minority programs. Harold Cruse suggests a special
responsibility for the black intellectual as he lays bare the hollowness
of much of the separatist rhetoric. "The Negro intellectual," he
writes, "must deal intimately with the power structure and cultural ap-
paratus, and the inner realities of the black world at the one and the
same time . . . he cannot be absolutely separated from either the black
or white world."

Earlier, W. E. B. DuBois described the black circumstance:
"Once and for all," he wrote, "let us realize that we are Americans,
that we were brought here with the earliest settlers and that the very
sort of civilization from which we came made the complete absorption
of Western modes and customs imperative if we were to survive at all;
in brief, there is nothing, so indigenous, so completely 'made in

America' as we. " More recently, Imamu Baraka added: "The paradox of the Negro experience in America is that it is a separate existence but inseparable from the complete fiber of American life . . . . In a sense history for the Negro before America must remain an emotional abstraction. " Such words are solemn, but much needed as restraints to those who are tempted, however understandably, to escape into an all-black world. We surrender our investment in the American experiment at great cost and at our own peril.

* * *

ROBERT C. WEAVER: Advocacy of black separatism is inevitable. It has been and is a reaction to the frustrations of racism and the dispair that follows. But it must be recognized also as a withdrawal or retreat; and paradoxically it achieves its greatest support at a time when the goal of integrationists—equal opportunity for competition—seems to be on the horizon. Separatism has had and continues to have a stifling impact upon the intellectual development and production of blacks; it also inhibits their economic progress.

Black Americans want and need knowledge of their heritage. To achieve this, they must comprehend the wider environment in which their experience occurred and upon which it exerted and continues to exert an impact. This requires knowing about pertinent African roots at the same time that there is recognition of significant events in America, the Caribbean, and thousands of communities where the black population lived and now resides. No less important is understanding of the economic, political and social institutions that developed and are developing in the larger society. To recognize these is to make meaningful the events that occurred and are occurring in the black community.

Preoccupation with blackness can be as misleading as a futile attempt to shun or ignore it. In a quest to identify our past, we must be hardheaded and realistic, rejecting romantic fiction. This does not imply abandonment or discrediting of African and black history. It simply dictates keeping them honest. If, in an attempt to correct the inaccuracies and omissions of the past, we substitute overstatements and unsupported fantasies, we replace one distortion by another. The goal is truth as far as it is achievable. That will be sufficient to instill a sense of ego identity, pride and self-knowledge in ourselves and our posterity.

The perils of separatism are not restricted to the world of ideas. In the current concentration of new employment opportunities out of the central city, it should be obvious that neither the ghetto nor the central city can afford sufficient jobs to meet the needs of urban blacks. Thus their movement into the suburbs becomes a necessity if they are to enjoy a solid economic base. This does not imply, however, that we abandon the concern for development of black entrepreneurship, but it and the nature of the American economy means that black economic separatism will not provide employment for the mass of black Americans.

Access of blacks to the total housing market has other benefits. It affords wider choices and mobility; it increases blacks' ability to achieve home ownership and affords them greater capacity to hedge against inflation, increase their savings, enjoy wider participation in federally-insured and guaranteed mortgages and associated economic benefits. Recognition of the need to break out of the restraints of racial residential segregation does not spell abandonment of the ghetto. In the first place, many areas of existing concentration of blacks are intrinsically desirable real estate and should be redeveloped, primarily for the present residents. Secondly, there is little likelihood that a significant number of blacks will soon escape from the ghetto, so that its occupants are rightly concerned with upgrading their existing neighborhoods. The issue is not a matter of either opening the suburbs or revitalizing the ghetto. Both processes are required, and each reinforces the other.

Just as blacks can best build and maintain a healthy self-image in an intellectual setting that recognizes their dual roles as Americans and blacks, so can they find an economic base only by simultaneously increasing their employment in the larger economy—often by securing free access to housing accessible to new job opportunities—and expanding black entrepreneurship.

Part One: The Separatism vs. Integration Controversy

Citations followed by an asterisk are annotated
in another chapter. Locate an annotation by
looking up the title in the index.

1. HISTORICAL PERSPECTIVES

The Beginnings 1760-1864

Allen, Robert. Black Awakening in Capitalist America: An Analytic History. Garden City, N.Y.: Doubleday, 1969.

The chapters "Black Nationalism and Black Power" and "Bourgeois Black Nationalism" discuss two separatist movements of the nineteenth century and the separatist philosophy of Roy Innis, national director of CORE.

Aptheker, Herbert. "Consciousness of Negro Nationality to 1900." In Toward Negro Freedom, pp. 104-11. New York: New Century Publishers, 1956.

This article traces the manifestation of Negro nationality in the United States, including those movements which advocated the founding of independent or quasi-independent republics in Texas and Oklahoma.

Bell, Howard H. "Expression of Negro Militancy in the North, 1840-1860." Journal of Negro History 45 (January 1960): 11-20.

Describes the growing mood of militancy among blacks in the North in the wake of the Fugitive Slave Law, the Kansas-Nebraska Act, and the Dred Scott decision, and the programs proposed. Among the spokesmen of the emigration movement were E. P. Walker, Martin R. Delany, and Henry Highland Garnet.

Blake, J. Herman. "Black Nationalism." Annals of the American Academy of Political and Social Science 382 (March 1969): 15-25.

Blake defines black nationalism and traces its origins in the early nineteenth century. He discusses the integration of political, economic, and cultural nationalism by Marcus Garvey after World War I, a religious dimension contributed by the Nation of Islam, and, in the contemporary period, the influence of Malcolm X.

3

Bracey, John H.; Meier, August; and Rudwick, Elliott; eds. Black Nationalism in America. Indianapolis: Bobbs-Merrill, 1970.

This collection of documents devoted to black nationalism includes selections from the writings of well-known nationalists and excerpts from speeches, leaflets, letters, black newspapers, and black conventions. Of special interest are: "Colonialization" (includes documents by Paul Cuffe, Daniel Coker, and Abraham Camp, and proceedings from the National Emigration Convention), "Territorial Separatism and Emigration," and "Black Capitalism."

Davis, Angela. "Reflections on the Black Woman's Role in the Community of Slaves." Black Scholar 3 (December 1971): 3-15.

A sketch of the resistance of slave women. Davis thinks that slavery forced black women to abandon passivity and fight for freedom with their men.

Delany, Martin R., and Campbell, Robert. Search For a Place; Black Separatism and Africa, 1860. Introduction by Howard H. Bell. Ann Arbor: University of Michigan Press, 1969.

A history of the separatist movement culminating in the effort to transfer American Negroes to Africa.

Dick, Robert C. "Rhetoric of Ante-bellum Black Separatism." Negro History Bulletin 34 (October 1971): 133-37.

Pragmatism and expediency remained the predominant values expressed by black spokesmen on separatism during the 1850s. An analysis of ante-bellum protest a decade earlier shows that the chief objective on the part of Negroes was integration.

Draper, Theodore. "The Fantasy of Black Nationalism." Commentary 48 (September 1969): 27-54.

A historical summary of American black nationalist movements, emphasizing territorial separatism in the eighteenth, nineteenth, and twentieth centuries. The Black Panthers were not in the line of pure black nationalist movements because their Marxist-Leninist orientation led to an emphasis on a social revolution by both blacks and whites. The Republic of New Africa is the purest black nationalist movement today.

Epps, Archie. "A Negro Separatist Movement of the Nineteenth Century." Harvard Review 4 (Summer 1969): 69-87.

Nineteenth- and twentieth-century separatist movements differ in style rather than ideology. This article describes nineteenth-century separatist activities in the African Methodist Episcopal

Church, the largest and oldest black church, whose history contrasts with the accepted view—put forth by E. Franklin Frazier and others—that black Christianity was characterized by passivity and lack of social concern.

Garrison, William Lloyd. Thoughts on African Colonization. Boston: Garrison and Knapp, 1832. Reprint. New York: Arno, 1969.

Garrison explains that he opposed the work of the American Colonization Society because it wanted to deport blacks rather than allow them to participate in American society.

Harding, Vincent. "Religion and Resistance Among Ante-bellum Negroes, 1800-1861." In The Making of Black America, edited by August Meier and Elliott Rudwick, 2 vols. Vol. 1, pp. 179-97. New York: Atheneum, 1969.

Christianity served slavery as a means of accommodating slaves to their life by sanctifying nonresistance and meekness. At the same time, it provided a means of resistance because religious meetings and services were used to organize and transmit information about slave escapes.

Harris, Sheldon H. Paul Cuffe: Black America and the African Return. New York: Simon and Schuster, 1972.

This biography of Cuffe, the emigrationist leader and antebellum colonizer, includes extracts from his journals and letters. Harris asserts that after Cuffe's death in 1817, no influential black leaders encouraged African resettlement until the post-Reconstruction era. Cuffe believed that although American slaves lived under intolerable conditions, they were better off than free Africans, who for the most part lacked contact with Christianity. He expected that if Africans became Christians, they would stop the slave trade, and full resettlement could then take place.

Hill, Adelaide Cromwell, and Kilson, Martin, eds. Apropos of Africa: Sentiments of Negro-American Leaders on Africa from the 1800s to the 1950s. London: Cass, 1969.

This anthology includes selections on emigration by Paul Cuffe, Martin Delany, Henry Turner; on Pan-Africanism by W. E. B. DuBois, Ralph Bunche, Canada Lee, A. Philip Randolph; and on the relation of American blacks in Africa. Several Pan-African organizations are described through excerpts from organizational material.

Lynch, Hollis R. "Pan-Negro Nationalism in the New World, Before 1862." In Boston University Papers on Africa, 2 vols. Vol. 2, pp. 149-79. Boston: Boston University Press, 1966.

This essay describes the early efforts and the rising nationalism that flourished among articulate blacks in the years before the Civil War.

McPherson, James M. "Abolitionist and Negro Opposition to Colonization During the Civil War." Phylon 26 (Winter 1965): 391-99.

The author describes the U. S. government role in the colonization movement. He concludes that, as a practical solution to the race question, colonization failed. White and black abolitionists believed that blacks would prefer to remain in America as second-class citizens rather than emigrate. Although blacks participated in these ill-fated schemes during the Civil War, most preferred to remain in the U. S. and fight for equality.

Payne, Daniel A. History of the African Methodist Episcopal Church. Nashville: Publishing House of the A. M. E. Sunday School Union, 1891.*

Pease, Jane H., and Pease, William H. "Black Power—the Debate in 1840." Phylon 29 (Spring 1968): 19-26.

In the 1840s blacks sought to fight for their rights collectively, and held conventions to plan their strategies. They disagreed on whether to rely on exclusively black support or to enlist the aid of whites. Some regarded the debate as reflecting inverse racism.

Pease, Jane H., and Pease, William H. "Organized Negro Communities: A North American Experiment." Journal of Negro History 47 (January 1962): 19-34.

A description of nineteenth-century black communities organized in response to discrimination and the benevolence of whites. The unresolved debate of integration versus isolation ultimately contributed to their demise.

Pease, William H., and Pease, Jane H. "The Negro Convention Movement." In Key Issues in the Afro-American Experience, edited by Nathan I. Huggins, Martin Kilson, and Daniel M. Fox, 2 vols. Vol. 1, pp. 191-205. New York: Harcourt Brace Jovanovich, 1971.

Blacks and white abolitionists held a series of national and local conventions in the 1830s. By 1840, white abolitionists were primarily interested in ending slavery, and because of the lack of

concern by whites for freed men and women, the convention movement developed a cohesive and distinctly black program, which the
authors see as being politically oriented and increasingly militant.
In the 1850s the movement drew many individuals who did not want
to be assimilated into American society; it culminated with the call
for separatism and emigration at the Cleveland convention in 1854.
Delany and Garnet used the conventions to voice their little-
supported demands for emigration.

Porter, Dorothy B. Early Negro Writing 1760-1837. Boston: Beacon,
    1971.

Selected writings which illustrate the forcefulness of leaders who
were engaged in efforts to emancipate the slaves and to improve
living conditions for free blacks, as well as debates about colonization and emigration.

Sherwood, Henry Noble. "Paul Cuffe." Journal of Negro History 8
    (April 1923): 153-232.

A biographical sketch of Paul Cuffe with an examination of his
emigration project to Sierra Leone and his attempts to establish
commercial ties there.

Stuckey, Sterling, ed. The Ideological Origins of Black Nationalism.
    Boston: Beacon, 1972.

In the introduction, Stuckey defines black nationalism as an ideology which emphasizes the need for black people to rely primarily
on themselves in economics, politics, religion, and culture. Most
nationalists wanted to explore possible solutions to slavery and
discrimination, and favored a return to Africa only as a last resort.
The anthology includes ante-bellum speeches and writings which
illustrate the editor's definition of nationalism. Among those rep-
resented are Henry Highland Garnet, Martin Delany, and William
Whipper.

Weisbord, Robert G. "The Back-to-Africa Idea." History Today 18
    (January 1968): 30-37.

The periodic revivals of the back-to-Africa theme occurred in
times of severe racial stress—just before the Civil War, in the
post-Reconstruction era, and in the aftermath of World War I.
Economic depression tended to aggravate racial discrimination.
A minority of blacks supported emigration; apathy and despair kept
many from emigrating.

Wesley, Charles. "Lincoln's Plan for Colonizing the Emancipated Negroes." Journal of Negro History 4 (January 1919): 7-18.

    Traces Lincoln's continuing support for Negro colonization
throughout his political career.

Whipper, William. "Opposition to Black Separatism." In The Ideological Origins of Black Nationalism, edited by Sterling Stuckey,
pp. 252-60. Boston: Beacon, 1972.

    Letters written in 1841 in response to the Albany Convention of
Colored Citizens in 1840. Whipper disagrees with the convention's
resolutions on the acceptance of segregation.

Reconstruction and After   1865-1953

Anderson, Arthur A. Prophetic Liberator of the Coloured Race of the
United States of America: Command to His People. New York:
New York Age Print, 1913.

    Advocates the formation of a separate state for a black nation, an
indemnity for slavery, and the unity of all colored peoples.

Bittle, William E., and Geis, Gilbert. The Longest Way Home: Chief
Alfred C. Sam's Back-to-Africa Movement. Detroit: Wayne State
University Press, 1964.

    The story of an early twentieth-century effort to establish an all-
Negro community in Oklahoma and in the Gold Coast.

Bittle, William E., and Geis, Gilbert. "Racial Self-Fulfillment and
the Rise of an All-Negro Community in Oklahoma." Phylon 18
(Third Quarter 1957): 247-60.

    An account of one of the early twentieth-century movements to
establish a black community in Oklahoma. The authors describe
the hopes and frustrations of the settlers and their subsequent attempts to create a home in Africa.

Blake, J. Herman. "Black Nationalism." Annals of the American
Academy of Political and Social Science 382 (March 1969): 15-25. *

Boyd, Willis Dolmond. "Negro Colonization in the Reconstruction Era,
1865-1870." Georgia Historical Quarterly 40 (December 1956):
360-82.

    This history of the colonization movement concludes that there was
little support from either whites or blacks for mass deportation,

whether voluntary or compulsory, and that the states themselves were powerless to enforce such a program. By 1870, the American Colonization Society had evolved into an educational and missionary organization, convinced that, in time, blacks would see the inevitability of a return to Africa.

Broderick, Francis L. "The Gnawing Dilemma: Separation and Integration, 1865-1925." In Key Issues in the Afro-American Experience, edited by Nathan I. Huggins, Martin Kilson, and Daniel M. Fox, 2 vols. Vol. 2, pp. 93-106. New York: Harcourt Brace Jovanovich, 1971.

Broderick describes events from Reconstruction to the post-World War I era, with attention to the work of Booker T. Washington, Frederick Douglass, W. E. B. DuBois, and Marcus Garvey.

Bunche, Ralph J. "A Critical Analysis of the Tactics and Programs of Minority Groups." Journal of Negro Education 4 (July 1935): 308-20.

Bunche discusses nonviolent tactics, including racial separatism, economic passive resistance, and economic separatism, as those methods black leadership has used most seriously in its efforts to free blacks from economic and political inequality. He concludes, however, that equality for minority groups will come through a reconstruction of American society by an alliance of black and white workers.

Bunche, Ralph J. "Extended Memorandum on the Programs, Ideologies, Tactics, and Achievements of Negro Betterment and Interracial Organizations." Vols. 2 and 3. July 7, 1940.

An analysis of the organizations devoting themselves to the betterment of the Negro. Back-to-Africa and chauvinist organizations are described and analyzed in volume 3: The Peace Movement of Ethiopia, the National Movement for the Forty-Ninth State and the UNIA.

Cronon, Edmund David. Black Moses. Madison: University of Wisconsin Press, 1955.

A biography of Marcus Garvey and a study of Garvey's Universal Negro Improvement Association, founded in 1918, which stimulated considerable enthusiasm for his plan to lead American Negroes back to Africa.

Douglass, Frederick. "Letter to W. J. Wilson, August 8, 1865." In
The Life and Writings of Frederick Douglass, edited by Philip S.
Foner, 4 vols. Vol. 4, pp. 171-74. New York: International Pub-
lishers, 1955.

In response to a letter seeking his aid for an "Educational Monument Association," a monument and college in honor of the memory of Abraham Lincoln, Douglas acknowledges the need for
educating colored people, but argues against creating schools to be
supported and attended solely by Negroes. "The spirit of the age
is against all institutions based upon prejudice," he wrote, "or
providing for prejudice of race. I, therefore, am opposed to doing
anything looking to the perpetuity of prejudice."

Douglass, Frederick. "The Present and Future of the Colored Race in
America." Speech delivered in the Church of the Puritans, New
York, May 1863. In The Life and Writings of Frederick Douglass,
edited by Philip S. Foner, 4 vols. Vol. 3, pp. 347-59. New York:
International Publishers, 1955.

The best solution for remedying problems of race relations in the
U. S. is to allow Negroes full civil and political equality.

DuBois, W. E. B. Dusk of Dawn: An Essay Toward an Autobiography
of a Race Concept. New York: Harcourt, 1940.

Distinguishes three categories of attempted solutions of the race
problem. First were the emigration movements, which attracted
some of the proudest and most independent blacks. The emigration schemes were killed in part by the lack of training and education of the ex-slaves, but were largely defeated by the industrial
expansion of Europe which made freedom and equality in Africa
unattainable. The second method, advocated by Booker T. Washington, was the self-segregation of black clubs or organizations,
neighborhoods, and schools. The third path, which DuBois advocates, consists of expanding the already existing separate black
economy, educational and religious organizations in the United
States so that their influence can be directed against exclusion
from mainstream society. The ultimate aim of this program
would be equal rights for black Americans. Economic organization is the most important part of the strategy because segregation
must first be broken down in its economic aspects.

DuBois, W. E. B. "Jim Crow." Crisis 17 (January 1919): 112-13.

A separate black America is described as impractical; yet the
author argues that if blacks are to develop their own gifts and
powers and if they are to bring about equality for all peoples, they
must unite and work together to build a new and great black ethos.

DuBois, W. E. B. "Strivings of the Negro People." Atlantic Monthly
80 (August 1897): 194-201.

An essay describing three decades of freedom for the American
Negro as being periods of conflict, of inspiration and of doubt—but
above all of hope that the principles of democracy will insure their
unrestricted acceptance into all areas of American life.

Frazier, E. Franklin. On Race Relations. Edited by G. Franklin
Edwards. Chicago: University of Chicago Press, 1968.

In an essay published in 1947, "Human, All Too Human: The Negro's Vested Interest in Segregation," Frazier points out that all
black institutions (churches, schools, hospitals, businesses)
flourished as a result of segregation. Black professionals face
less competition in such limited work, and may resist social
change on selfish grounds. Those whose status might suffer in an
integrated society frequently resist change on the grounds of racial
pride and belief in the psychological importance of black institutions. Also, those blacks who serve as mediators between black
and white societies would lose their function in an integrated society.

Garvey, Marcus. "Aims and Objects of Movement for Solution of
Negro Problems." In Philosophy and Opinions of Marcus Garvey,
edited by Amy Jacques Garvey, 2 vols. Vol. 2, pp. 37-43. New
York: Universal Publishing House, 1925.

The efforts of groups to encourage integration of the races have
caused much trouble for blacks in the United States. The program of the UNIA seeks to perpetuate racial purity and pride, and
to encourage blacks to work together in establishing their own institutions and a home for all black people in Africa.

Garvey, Marcus. "The True Solution of the Negro Problem." In
Philosophy and Opinions of Marcus Garvey, edited by Amy Jacques
Garvey, 2 vols. Vol. 1, pp. 52-53. New York: Universal Publishing
House, 1923.

In this statement Garvey advocates reclaiming Africa for all black
peoples of the earth.

Grimke, Francis J. "Colored Men as Professors in Colored Institutions." A. M. E. Church Review 4 (July 1885): 142-49.

A Presbyterian minister and protest leader of Washington, D. C.,
argues in part for greater black control of educational institutions.

Higgins, Chester. "Group of Intellectuals Were Fed Up with Maltreatment." Jet 34 (May 30, 1968): 14-21.

In 1933 a group of black men and women under the leadership of Oscar C. Brown, Sr. proposed the establishment of Texas as the forty-ninth state where blacks could work out their own destiny. Brown still believes that the plan, never implemented, is a viable solution to the race problem.

Hill, Adelaide Cromwell and Kilson, Martin, eds. Apropos of Africa: Sentiments of Negro-American Leaders on Africa from the 1800s to the 1950s. London: Cass, 1969. *

Hill, Mozell C. "The All-Negro Communities of Oklahoma: The Natural History of a Social Movement." Journal of Negro History 31 (July 1946): 254-68.

This study discusses the similarities and differences of the great westward march by blacks and whites, the racial polarization on the frontier, and compares the all-Negro community movement in Oklahoma with other nationalist Negro movements which occurred at the turn of the century.

Johnson, Guy B. "Some Factors in the Development of Negro Social Institutions in the United States." American Journal of Sociology 30 (November 1934): 329-37.

Cultural isolation, race prejudice, and economic drag have stimulated the development of those black institutions that offer opportunities for leadership and self-expression within the group, particularly the church and the lodge. Since Emancipation, race consciousness has given rise to various agencies for racial solidarity, the black press being the most important. In view of the increasing likeness of white and black culture, there can be no possibility of blacks creating a unique type of culture in the United States.

Johnson, James Weldon. Negro Americans, What Now? New York: Viking, 1934.

An examination of the major ideological alternatives advocated by various blacks, e.g., exodus, physical force, revolution, isolationism, and integration. Creating an "imperium in imperio" is not any easier or more feasible as a means to achieving full equality than striving for an end to involuntary segregation. Furthermore, even if isolationism were used as a tactic, it is possible that blacks would arouse additional envy and hatred and be subjected to more persecution by the majority. In order to achieve full rights, blacks must simultaneously make involuntarily imposed segregated institutions the very best they can be, and strive for integrated institutions.

Moore, Richard B. "Africa Conscious Harlem." In Harlem: A Community in Transition, edited by John Henrik Clarke, pp. 77-96. New York: Citadel, 1964.

A history of Pan-Africanism in Harlem with emphasis on the various back-to-Africa movements and a discussion of the chief intellectual forces that encouraged interest in Africa during the 1930s.

Obatala, J. K. "Exodus: Black Zionism." Liberator 9 (October 1969): 14-17.

Describes the spontaneous, nationalist-agrarian movement of blacks to Kansas in the late 1870s.

Palmer, Edward N. "Negro Secret Societies." Social Forces 23 (December 1944): 207-12.

During the post-Emancipation period, many blacks readily accepted secret societies as economic and social cooperation was the only way to survive. The secret societies tended to duplicate institutions in which blacks were denied participation. Their establishment indicates that blacks saw themselves as an integral part of American society.

Plessy v. Ferguson, 163 U.S. 537(1896).

The United States Supreme Court upheld the constitutionality of an 1890 act of the state of Louisiana requiring separate accommodations for black and white passengers. The majority argued that laws requiring separation of the races does not necessarily imply the inferiority of either race; therefore state legislatures and courts of states can exercise such rulings.

Randolph, A. Philip. "The Only Way to Redeem Africa." The Messenger 5 (1923): 568-70, 612-14. Reprinted in Black Power: The Radical Response to White America, edited by Thomas Wagstaff, pp. 87-97. Beverly Hills: Glencoe, 1969.

Randolph argues against Garveyism on the grounds that European countries with economic interests in Africa would not allow emigrants to set up an expatriate nation there. In any case, Garvey's supporters would not have the skills to do so. Africa's problems are economic; it can be redeemed only when the capitalist system which exploits it for raw materials is overthrown. In contrast, political power is the fundamental need for American blacks.

Randolph, A. Philip. "Why Should We March?" Survey Graphic
31 (November 1942): 488-89.

Written immediately before the first March on Washington by
blacks, Randolph points out that the March is all-Negro, but not
anti-white. It is being held to demonstrate black mass power.

Redding, J. Saunders. On Being Negro in America. Indianapolis:
Bobbs-Merrill, 1951.

A book-length essay on Redding's perceptions of the race problem
in America. His position is that of an integrationist. "Race
chauvinism" is counter-productive because it is a narrow, limiting conviction based on emotional needs. He also comments on
the role of Communism vs. democracy in the struggle of American
blacks to achieve their rights.

Redkey, Edwin S. Black Exodus, Black Nationalism and Back-to-
Africa Movements, 1890-1910. New Haven: Yale University
Press, 1969.

A detailed account of the reasons for, and the fate of, several back-
to-Africa schemes in the late nineteenth and early twentieth centuries.

Reynolds, Alfred W. "The Alabama Negro Colony in Mexico; 1894-
96." Alabama Review 5 (October 1952): 243-68; 6 (January 1953):
31-58.

The story of the Alabama Negro Colony in Mexico, the first large-
scale migration of blacks into Mexico. It failed miserably, and because of poor conditions, many of the 816 blacks tried to escape.
Eventually their plight was recognized by the U.S. government,
which set up a quarantine camp and organized transportation back
to the U.S.

Rippy, J. Fred. "A Negro Colonization Project in Mexico, 1895."
Journal of Negro History 6 (January 1921): 66-73.

A descriptive account of a private project to colonize blacks in
Mexico.

Schwedmann, Glen. "St. Louis and the 'Exodusters' of 1879." Journal of Negro History 46 (January 1961): 32-46.

An analysis of the social and political conditions in the South that
stimulated the migration of black farmers to Kansas.

Sherwood, Henry Noble. "Early Negro Deportation Projects." Mississippi Valley Historical Review 2 (March 1916): 484-508.

The movement to colonize blacks was integral to the emancipation
movement of the abolitionists during the 1800s. Most abolitionists
believed that dissension and strife would result if the freed Negroes
remained among the whites. The author discusses schemes by
Craighead, Fairfax, Jefferson, Samuel Hopkins, and others, for
deportation, either back to Africa (to serve as missionaries, for
example) or to an unsettled area in the U.S. Expense was the
major obstacle to emigration.

Tolson, Arthur. "Oklahoma's All-Black State Movement, 1889-1907."
Black Collegian 2 (March-April 1972): 8-10, 48.

A description of the Oklahoma Immigration Society's all-black
state plan headed by Edward P. McCabe to encourage black migration to the twin territories. Despite the use of agents in the
South and the support of certain influential whites in the Republican
party, the scheme failed.

Trotter, William Monroe. [Profile] In Harvard College, Class of
1895. Thirtieth Annual Report, no. 7, p. 303. Cambridge, Mass.:
The University Press, 1925.

Trotter, a black Harvard graduate, explains his reasons for founding the pro-integration newspaper, the Guardian, and for opposing
all compromise on racial issues, including the gradualism of
Booker T. Washington.

Wahle, Kathleen O. "Alexander Crummell: Black Evangelist."
Phylon 29 (Winter 1968): 388-95.

During the last third of the nineteenth century, Alexander Crummell supported the efforts of American blacks to improve the race
through their own efforts. He advocated emigration to Africa and
worked toward this end from the 1850s to 1870s. The author
points out that Crummell emphasized civil rights and power
through character development and separate racial organization.

Washington, Booker T. Address delivered at the opening of the Cotton
States and International Exposition at Atlanta, Georgia, September 18, 1895.

Washington's solution to the race problem, especially the question
of social equality, is expressed in the statement: "in all things
that are purely social we can be as separate as the fingers, yet
one as the hand in all things essential to mutual progress."

Washington, Booker T. The Future of the American Negro. New York: Negro Universities Press, 1969.

First published in 1899, this book summarizes Washington's views on race relations. He did not think that emigration to Africa was possible for more than a few individuals. Education was seen as the primary goal, as the means of enabling blacks to serve the black community first, and then to compete in the white business world.

Weinstein, James, ed. "Black Nationalism: The Early Debate." Studies on the Left 4 (Summer 1964): 50-58.

In an interview in 1920, Marcus Garvey said: "We believe in the U. S. Constitution for the Americans, but we stand for the idea of Africa for the Africans. It is not our intention or purpose to send all Negroes back to Africa." His position is rebutted by Chandler Owen and A. Philip Randolph, editors of The Messenger, and by W. E. B. DuBois.

Weisbord, Robert G. "The Back-to-Africa Idea." History Today 18 (January 1968): 30-37. *

White, Walter. "Segregation—a Symposium." Crisis 41 (March 1934): 80-81.

White describes his position in response to W. E. B. DuBois's editorials on segregation in issues of Crisis. Accepting the status of separateness in any form, whether voluntarily or imposed, means inferior accommodations. "The Negro must, without yielding, continue the grim struggle for integration and against segregation for his own physical, moral and spiritual well-being and for that of white America and of the world at large."

Woodson, Carter G. A Century of Negro Migration. Washington, D. C.: Association for the Study of Negro Life and History, 1918.

A review prepared for the layman incorporating information on the migration of blacks up to World War I.

2. THE TWENTY YEARS SINCE BROWN

Allen, Robert. Black Awakening in Capitalist America: An Analytic
   History. Garden City, N.Y.: Doubleday, 1969.*

Anderson, S.E. "The Fragmented Movement." Negro Digest 17 (September-October 1968): 4-10.

   Contemporary roads to black liberation fall into five major factions:
   "the integrationist, the city-statesman, back-to-Africaism, the
   black nation concept, and the revolutionary nationalism." The
   author concludes that blacks must lead the way to enforce changes
   and to rebuild America in terms of racial equality.

Baldwin, James. "East River, Downtown: Postscript to a Letter from Harlem." In Nobody Knows My Name, pp. 72-82. New York: Dial, 1961.

   In this essay, first published under the title "A Negro Assays the
   Negro Mood" in the New York Times Magazine in 1961, Baldwin
   assesses the views of blacks who are not firmly committed to integration. He points out that the primary allegiance of American
   blacks must be to America, but that there is a logic in the Black
   Muslims' reluctance to be contributing members of American society, which Baldwin views as corrupt.

Baldwin, James. "A Letter to Americans." Freedomways 8 (Spring
   1968): 112-16.

   The concept of black power, which Baldwin says accompanied the
   first African slaves to America, was resurrected, not created, by
   Stokely Carmichael. The white backlash is simply the reaction of
   whites to the revitalization of the black power ideology. Baldwin
   states that Western self-interest and black self-interest are irrec-
   oncilable, but that Carmichael represents a new generation of
   blacks who will force America to change, or will destroy themselves in the process.

Baldwin, James. No Name in the Street. New York: Dial, 1972, pp.
   90-100, passim.

   Includes in loosely organized form reminiscences of Malcolm X
   and Martin Luther King in which they are viewed as more alike
   than different. Baldwin believes that both men began to see that

the nature of white America's indifference and racism toward the black man had to be revealed, not just to save black people, but to change the world in which everyone has to live.

Baraka, Imamu Amiri. Kawaida Studies: The New Nationalism. Chicago: Third World Press, 1972.

Four of these six essays, interpretations of the ideas of Maulana Ron Karenga, were originally published in journals. Central concepts are Pan-Africanism and the need for black political, religious, social, economic, ethical, creative, and historical institutions.

Baraka, Imamu Amiri. Raise Race Rays Raze: Essays Since 1965. New York: Vintage, 1971.

These essays on social and aesthetic matters are generally theoretical. Regarding separatism, Baraka states in "Raise #3, Presidents," that blacks will be slaves of white nations until they establish their own black nations. In "The Need for a Cultural Base to Civil Rites and Bpower Mooments" he says that "Black power, as an actuality, will only exist in a Black-oriented, Black-controlled space." He advocates the establishment of schools to teach black consciousness on a community level and the takeover of Negro colleges to teach nationalism.

Baraka, Imamu Amiri. "Toward Ideological Clarity." Black World 24 (November 1974): 24-33+.

The historical background and contemporary manifestations of the Afro-American struggle for liberation. The author proposes an ideology based on nationalism, Pan-Africanism, and socialism to be used against racism in a three-point program: acquisition and redistribution of power and the unification of Third World peoples.

Baraka, Imamu Amiri. "What Does Nonviolence Mean? In the Face of War and Death." Negro Digest 13 (October 1964): 4-19.

Baraka sets forth his growing disenchantment with nonviolence; he believes that whites will use the nonresistance of blacks as an excuse for genocide. He also states that the civil rights movement failed to help most blacks; it benefited only the middle class, which is primarily interested in preserving the status quo.

Baskin, Darryl. "Black Separatism." Journal of Higher Education 40 (December 1969): 731-34.

It is unreasonable to define black separatism as segregation. Rather, it is argued here, black separatism is a pluralist stratagem designed to define a culture free of white interference.

Bennett, Lerone, Jr. "Liberation." Ebony 25 (August 1970): 36-43.

> The author espouses the philosophy of liberation in dealing with the problem of black-white relations in the U.S. He argues that the choices of integration or separatism are false ones, for blacks may have to utilize both or neither to achieve equality. Liberation, he asserts, is the means toward transformation or creation of a single human community in this country.

Billings, Charles E. "Black Activists and the Schools." High School Journal 54 (November 1970): 96-107.

> Reports the results of a questionnaire given to activist and non-activist black high school students which showed that fewer than one-fourth of each group favored racial separation.

"Birth of a (Black) Nation." Esquire 71 (January 1969): 70-77.

> A discussion of the growing movement to form a black nation within the United States through interviews with the president of the Republic of New Africa, Robert F. Williams, and his cabinet. These individuals reject their United States citizenship and claim five southern states for the creation of the new nation. Illustrated.

"Black Nationalists' Plan for Splitting of 5 States." Jet 34 (April 11, 1968): 9.

> The separatist Malcolm X Society proposes the creation of an independent black-controlled nation carved from five southern states.

"The Black Neo-Segregationists." Crisis 74 (November 1967): 439-40.

> This editorial decries the rise of black separatism. While the majority of American blacks reject segregation and continue to fight for the right to compete on an equal basis in all areas of American life, there are some who espouse separatism. These neo-segregationists, insecure and fearful in a competitive society, are now calling for other blacks to join them in seeking the unrealistic promises of self-segregation.

Blake, J. Herman. "Black Nationalism." Annals of the American Academy of Political and Social Science 382 (March 1969): 15-25. *

Borghese, Elizabeth Mann. "The Other Hill." Center Magazine 1 (July 1968): 2-11.

> The author opposes the creation of a separate "Black Nation," but proposes self-managing black communities throughout the country. A separate educational system would be the foundation of

these communities. Members would be elected to a Diet which would face Congress on "The Other Hill, " and coordinate the policies of all self-managing black communities.

Bracey, John H.; Meier, August; and Rudwick, Elliott; eds. Black Nationalism in America. Indianapolis: Bobbs-Merrill, 1970.*

Breitman, George. By Any Means Necessary. New York: Pathfinder Press, 1970.

A collection of speeches and interviews made by Malcolm X during his last year. They reflect Malcolm's new interest in the common bond between oppressed people in Asia, Africa, and the United States.

Broderick, Francis L. "The Gnawing Dilemma: Separatism and Integration, 1865-1925. " In Key Issues in the Afro-American Experience, edited by Nathan I. Huggins, Martin Kilson, and Daniel M. Fox, 2 vols. Vol. 2, pp. 93-106. New York: Harcourt Brace Jovanovich, 1971.*

Brown et al. v. Board of Education of Topeka et al. 347 U.S. 483(1954). In Argument: The Oral Argument Before the Supreme Court in Brown v. Board of Education of Topeka, 1952-55, edited by Leon Friedman, pp. 325-31. New York: Chelsea House, 1969.*

Browne, Robert S. "The Case for Black Separatism. " Ramparts 6 (December 1967): 46-51.

The Conference on Black Power, held in Newark, New Jersey in 1967, passed a resolution calling for a national dialogue on the desirability of partitioning the United States into two separate, independent nations. Browne states that the intent of the resolution was to begin a reasoned discussion of the question, since no one knows the number of blacks who would support a partitioned U.S. Browne postulates that neither nation would be overtly racist; separation would remove the cause for animosity.

Browne, Robert S. "The Case for Two Americas—One Black, One White, " New York Times Magazine, 11 August 1968, pp. 12-13+.

Browne asserts that the black community does not have a homogeneous view of its predicament. Thus, strategies of separatism and integration coexist. Browne agrees with advocates of partition, who believe that American blacks as a cultural group are ethnically distinct from the majority culture. Whether a black person is an integrationist or a separatist is determined by his or her position on the issue of cultural difference.

Browne, Robert S. "Separation. " Ebony 25 (August 1970): 46-52.

Browne argues that the history of the black man in the United States has shown that integration should not be the sole route to liberation

Browne considers the possibility of black control of one or more of the existing state governments in order to achieve black liberation.

Browne, Robert S., and Rustin, Bayard. Separatism or Integration: Which Way for America? New York: A. Philip Randolph Institute, 1968.

Browne considers the challenge to integrate as a psychological problem: more fortunate blacks have been absorbed into the dominant culture only to ignore their African heritage. Integration also perpetuates white control of the black community. These identity problems indicate to Browne that partition would offer the best solution. Rustin emphasizes that the problems of blacks are a class problem and that the solution is a midway position between separatism and integration. Black pride and black institutions should be developed and, at the same time, blacks should work to create integration.

Browne, Robert S.; Lynch, Hollis R.; and Wright, Major. "Three Writers on the Question of Repatriation." Freedomways 8 (Summer 1968): 255-61.

Browne suggests consideration of both repatriation and partition as viable alternatives for black America. Lynch believes that, first, black Americans must recognize the feasibility and desirability of a considered repatriation scheme. Major Wright states that going to Africa does not make an individual safe from racial oppression or economic exploitation.

Carmichael, Stokely. Stokely Speaks: Black Power Back to Pan-Africanism. New York: Vintage, 1971.

A collection of Carmichael's articles and speeches from 1965 to 1971, presented in chronological order, demonstrating his ideological development. In the most recent article, on Pan-Africanism, he advocates the return of all African people to the motherland.

Carter, Robert L. "The Role of the Black Lawyer in Today's Black Revolution." Humanist 28 (September-October 1969): 5-11.

Carter encourages black lawyers to reassert themselves and to propose new civil rights legislation primarily for the moral uplift of black people. He does not consider this a separatist position since he does not deny that white lawyers can contribute to the struggle.

Clark, Kenneth B. "The Booby Trap of Black Separatism." Speech delivered at the University of Chicago, May 1972.

A discussion of the dilemma caused by American racism and an analysis of one of the most dramatic manifestations of this dilemma—the demand by blacks for self-segregation and separatism. "Booby traps" include semantic separatism, as indicated by the term "black" to describe Negro Americans; the demand by black students for separate living facilities, special departments, and black studies courses; and the emergence of black professional groups, e. g. , black sociologists, black psychologists. Because these separatist trends imitate the "atavistic idiocies" of white organizations, they are not contributing to the demise of racial segregation and discrimination.

Clark, Kenneth B. "The Negro and the Urban Crisis." In Agenda for the Nation, edited by Kermit Gordon, pp. 124-40. Garden City, N. Y.: Doubleday, 1968.

The contemporary pattern of race relations in American cities is characterized by intensified social disruption by blacks and increasing resistance and negative response from whites. One of the results of the urban racial dilemma is the separatist movement, a rejection of racial integration, which has failed as the experience of antipoverty programs demonstrates. These programs fail when they become identified with blacks rather than with a movement to rebuild the city as a whole. The problems of the cities and of the relationships between Negroes and whites are inextricably woven. A comprehensive plan that takes this into account is required if our cities are to survive.

Clark, Kenneth B. "The Negro Elected Public Official in the Changing American Scene." Speech delivered at the National Conference of Negro Elected Officials, Chicago, September 30, 1967. *

Clark, Kenneth B. Prejudice and Your Child. Boston: Beacon, 1963.

A discussion for laymen of the factors in our society that stimulate, perpetuate, and reinforce negative racial attitudes in children as determined by social science research, clinical data, theoretical analyses, and general observations. A suggested plan of action for schools, social agencies, churches, and parents is given to help them reevaluate and modify their programs and attitudes.

Clark, Kenneth B. "Thoughts on Black Power." Dissent 15 (March-April 1968): 98, 192.

Black power is generally not seen by its proponents as an interim phase toward racial justice and it is certainly not proposed as a step toward racial integration. Segregation demanded by Negroes will be no more beneficial than segregation imposed by whites.

Clark, Kenneth B. "Where It's At: Civil Rights." Vogue 151 (April 1, 1968): 178-79+.

A discussion of the slogan "Black Power" and its effect on the civil rights movement. Clark writes, "The Black Power

movement is ambiguous, irrational, and inconsistent and attempts
to make a virtue out of racial segregation. It feeds on the negative
realities of the predicament of the Negro in American life, on the
widespread anger, despair, and sense of hopelessness which came
in the wake of tokensim, white backlash, and the persistent unfulfilled promises of racial progress." The rhetoric of black power,
however, has made American whites aware of the nature of racism.

Cleage, Albert B., Jr. "A Black Man's View of Authority." In <u>Evasion
of Authority</u>, edited by Clyde L. Manschreck, pp. 59-91. Nashville: Abingdon, 1971.

Integration is "the name given to the black man's philosophy of
self-hate and the dream of integration is the mechanism by which
black people permit themselves to be controlled." Since the white
power structure created a separate society, blacks can utilize this
separateness as a basis for political and economic power as well
as "for the transmission of cultural values."

Cohen, Robert Carl. <u>Black Crusader: A Biography of Robert Franklin
Williams</u>. Secaucus, N.J.: Lyle Stuart, 1972.

This book, primarily based on tape-recorded conversations between the author and Willaims, is an account of Williams's meta-
morphosis into an "archenemy" of American social and economic
policies who advocates armed self-defense for black people.

Cruse, Harold. <u>The Crisis of the Negro Intellectual</u>. New York:
William Morrow, 1967.

The author contends that the history of the Negro in America is
dominated by the conflict between integrationist and nationalist
forces in economics, politics, and culture. The Negro intellectual has failed to understand the historical basis of these forces and
to reconcile them effectively.

De Barry, Clyde E.; Fashing, Joseph; and Harris, Calvin. "Black
Power and Black Population: A Dilemma." <u>Journal of Negro Edu-
cation</u> 38 (Winter 1969): 14-21.

A report of a survey conducted in Eugene, Oregon, to determine
whether or not members of the black community were integrated
more successfully in community life than in cities with larger per-
centages of blacks. Blacks had not been as readily integrated into
the community life and activities of Eugene as in cities with more
Negroes. CORE and NAACP have been effective in helping blacks
to realize that if changes are to be made, they cannot wait for the
white community to make them.

"A Dialogue on Separatism." Ebony 25 (August 1970): 62-70.

> Jesse L. Jackson and Alvin F. Poussaint agree that nationalism
> and black-controlled institutions must precede integration. They
> emphasize the need for blacks to work first toward a "psycholog-
> ical nation" (self-love, pride, solidarity); perhaps then economic
> and political power will come about.

Drake, St. Clair. "Prospects for the Future." In Key Issues in the
   Afro-American Experience, edited by Nathan I. Huggins, Martin
   Kilson, and Daniel M. Fox, 2 vols. Vol. 2, pp. 280-302. New
   York: Harcourt Brace Jovanovich, 1971.

> Drake asserts that the integration-separation antithesis does not
> reflect contemporary reality. Impermeable boundaries cannot be
> maintained except for a small portion of the population. Militant
> rhetoric will dissolve quickly. Martin Luther King's centrist ap-
> proach was the appropriate method to achieve racial integration.
> Since this is the opinion of most blacks and the black-white liberal
> coalition, it will gradually be successful.

Draper, Theodore. "The Fantasy of Black Nationalism." Commentary 48 (September 1969): 27-54. *

Ellison, Ralph. Shadow and Act. New York: Random House, 1964.

> This collection includes essays largely dating from the 1940s and
> 1950s. In an interview from Preuves, Ellison remarks that
> American blacks are the only nonwhite minority in the world to be
> fighting for fuller participation in the shared society, not for sep-
> aration. The desegregation movement is a manifestation of in-
> creasing awareness of the values of black culture. He expects
> that, as integration increases, blacks will value group expression
> all the more.

Essien-Udom, E. U. Black Nationalism: The Search for an Identity in
   America. Chicago: University of Chicago Press, 1962. *

Essien-Udom, E. U. "The Nationalist Movements of Harlem." In
   Harlem: A Community in Transition, edited by John Henrik
   Clarke. New York: Citadel, 1964.

> The discussion centers on contemporary partition, emigration,
> and separation schemes.

Feagin, Joe R. "White Separatists and Black Separatists: A Comparative Analysis." Social Problems 19 (Fall 1971): 167-80.

> "This paper focuses on certain extreme separatist models pro-
> posed in regard to black-white adjustment, first by examining

the historical background, then by reanalyzing recent survey data to assess the extent to which rank-and-file white and black Americans support separatist solutions." The author's analysis of the survey data indicates that there is strong support for separatism by whites and an overwhelming rejection by blacks of extreme versions of separatism.

Ferry, William H. "Black Colonies: A Modest Proposal." Center Magazine 1 (January 1968): 74-76.

Integration is not working and not wanted by most whites and some blacks, so this author proposes the formal establishment of a system of black colonies in the United States.

Franklin, John Hope. "The Two Worlds of Race: A Historical View." Daedalus 94 (Fall 1965): 899-920.

A part of this essay considers why some blacks wish to perpetuate a dual society. Two reasons are vested interests in their own institutions and a sincere commitment to the advantages of cultural pluralism. This separatist trend, however, is difficult to maintain against other forces working to eliminate all-black institutions.

Galamison, Milton A. "Integration Must Work—Nothing Else Can." Freedomways 3 (Spring 1963): 215-17.

An impassioned statement against separatism, arguing that all Americans share the responsibility for American cultural and political institutions.

Gershman, Carl. "Black Separatism: Shock of Integration." Dissent 17 (July-August 1969): 294-97.

In this discussion of separatist trends among college students, the shock of integration and the bitterness caused by discrimination are cited as the major reasons for the separatist mood among working class and middle-class black students. Thought most blacks are not separatist, they are angry and frustrated. The explosiveness of this situation can be headed off by political integration and economic equality.

Goldman, Peter. The Death and Life of Malcolm X. New York: Harper and Row, 1973.

In this biographical account that focuses on the death and legacy of Malcolm X, Goldman points out that Malcolm preached separatism while he was a Black Muslim. Even after his break with that organization in 1964, he maintained his belief that separatism was the only ultimate solution, and argues that blacks' economic and social needs could not wait for fulfillment until a new nation was established.

Hahn, Harlan. "Black Separatists: Attitudes and Objectives in a Riot-torn Ghetto." Journal of Black Studies 1 (September 1970): 35-53.*

Hamilton, Charles V. "The Nationalist vs. the Integrationist." New York Times Magazine, 3 October 1972, pp. 36-38+.

A discussion of the differences in beliefs and strategies between nationalists and integrationists. The author doubts that a rap-prochement can never be worked out between the two groups, but they should be able to unite on certain neutral issues, e.g., nar-cotics, full employment, improved health care, and adequate hous-ing.

Handlin, Oscar. Fire-Bell in the Night: The Crisis in Civil Rights. Boston: Beacon, 1964.

An assessment of the civil rights movement ten years after Brown. The gains of nonviolent protest will be lost unless full equality is attained. American society must function as a pluralist one, in which each racial or cultural group has access to political and economic power, or it will revert to apartheid. Handlin sees black nationalism as a potentially significant threat to pluralism because its adherents do not deal with what he views as their real problems.

Harding, Vincent. "Black Radicalism: The Road from Montgomery." In Dissent: Explorations in the History of American Radicalism, edited by Alfred F. Young, pp. 319-54. DeKalb, Ill.: Northern Illinois University Press, 1968.

Every generation has included black radicals who have moved be-yond acceptable or customary lines of protest and revolt. The usual goal of the radicals has been assimilation into a reformed American society. Only those who do not seek assimilation can be considered nationalists. Thus, the transformation of black radi-cals into nationalists which took place in the late 1960s was in keeping with historical precedents. Harding traces the element of nationalism in members of SCLC and SNCC and in Malcolm X. By 1964 Malcolm had rejected separatism, but was never able to ac-cept integration in its place.

Henderson, Vivian W. Text of Address for Plans of Progress College Relations Conference. Atlanta, April 29, 1968.

Henderson accepts the concept of black power when it refers to economic and political viability and pride in the black heritage, but he strongly disagrees with those who call for separatism as a permanent solution or as a means to achieve a pluralistis society. Separatism, he says, would be readily accepted by whites who would use it to keep down blacks.

Hill, Adelaide Cromwell. "The Dilemma of the Afro-American." Afro-American Studies 2 (December 1971): 187-89.

Hill states that leaders of the black revolution are asking blacks to create a new system, based on a sense of history, withdrawal, violence, and self-determination. She believes that violence may be unavoidable, although sense of history and self-determination have positive connotations; but that withdrawal and separation are unrealistic on any terms, particularly when based on historical-cultural values.

Howard, John R. The Cutting Edge: Social Movements and Social Change in America. Philadelphia: Lippincott, 1974.

In his historical, theoretical, and empirical discussion of various movements for change by blacks in America, Howard points out that separatism is one of the post-riot era trends. Contemporary separatism rests on three assumptions: racism is an indelible part of the white psyche; blacks have certain common characteristics arising largely out of the shared experience of oppression and exploitation; and a separate sovereignty is the only alternative for blacks.

Hunter, Charlayne. "Black Intellectuals Divided over Ideological Directions." New York Times, 28 April 1975, pp. 1, 57.

An overview of the current ideological debate among black intellectuals and activists on the role of color, class and economic status in the racial oppression of black people.

"Integrated or Separate: Which Road to Progress?" New Generation 49 (Fall 1967): 1-28.

The issue is devoted to pro and con arguments on the strategies of integration vs. separatism to win economic and political equality for black people. On education, Roy Innis and Victor Solomon call for the establishment of separate institutions for black Americans and specifically for an autonomous Harlem school district. Dan Dodson disagrees with this. Frances Fox Piven, Clarence Funnye, Preston Wilcox, Kenneth Simmons, and Conrad Lynn contribute other points of view to the dialogue on housing and political action.

"Interview with John Hope Franklin, " Urban Review 5 (September 1971): 32-
37. *

Isaacs, Harold R. "Integration and the Negro Mood. " Commentary 34
(December 1962): 487-97.

An analysis of the ways in which alienation, assimilation, and integration have shaped the identity of the Negro in America. There
has always been a fringe of cults which served as psychological out-
lets for the alienated black—for example, Garveyism, Father Divine,
the Black Muslims. Blacks who support these extremist philosophies,
as well as those who are less fundamentally alienated, must bridge
the gap between their identification as Americans and as non-
Americans before equality can be achieved.

Jordon, Vernon E. "The New Civil Rights Struggle. " Essence 2 (February 1972): 36-37.

In spite of the achievements of the civil rights era, the record re-
veals a mixed pattern of progress and setbacks for American blacks.
Those with skills and education have progressed, but educational and
economic gaps have widened between whites and the masses of blacks.
The task of the seventies is to implement those rights won in the
sixties and to develop economic and political power for all blacks.
This goal will require a new strategy: that of building broad coalitions for gaining the necessary political power to bring about change.

King, Martin Luther. "Letter from Birmingham Jail. " April 16, 1963,
20 pages.

An affirmation of the philosophy and the nonviolent, direct action
strategy of civil disobedience against enforced segregation and a
denial that the activities of the Southern Christian Leadership Conference are extremist. Rather, King argues, his movement stands
in the middle of two opposing forces: the "do-nothingism of the
complacent" and the "hatred and despair of the black nationalist. "

King, Martin Luther. The Trumpet of Conscience. New York: Harper
and Row, 1967.

These talks were broadcast in 1967 as the Massey Lectures over
the Canadian Broadcasting Corporation. Speaking of the crisis
intensified by the riots, King says that blacks disagree about the
methods to be used in rebuilding American society while agreeing
that equality is the goal.

King, Martin Luther. Where Do We Go From Here: Chaos or Community? Boston: Beacon, 1968.

King visualises the future of the civil rights movement as

necessitating involvement in many facets of the complex struggle for black equality. The concept of black political, economic, and psychological power is central to black equality, but the slogan "Black Power" connotes black domination. He denies that separatism is a viable alternative; political and economic alliances must be formed with white society, but black unity must also be maintained.

Kirschenmann, Frederick. "The Danger and Necessity of Black Separatism." <u>Lutheran Quarterly</u> 21 (November 1969): 352-57.

The author points out the dangers of black separatism, but suggests that there are necessary risks at this time because blacks must have the opportunity to recover the roots of their culture. Integration is not to be merely assimilation. Whites must resist the urge to retreat into enclaves, remain open to the possibility of straight talk with separatists, and develop relations with blacks who do not identify with the separatist movement. Whites must also make a major effort to root out their own prejudice.

Koontz, Elizabeth. "Complete Integration Must Be the Goal." <u>Ebony</u> 26 (August 1970): 138-41.

"Separatism is a philosophy of self-defeating desperation, and worse, it flies in the face of reality in a world crying out for a new morality in social leadership."

Ladner, Joyce, ed. <u>The Death of White Sociology.</u> New York: Vintage, 1973.

The editor states in the introduction that this anthology was organized to distinguish black sociology from white sociology, and to define concepts and theories which utilize the experiences and histories of black Americans. Black sociology has evolved as an outgrowth of and a reaction to the biases of mainstream sociology, which writes about blacks as a culture deviant from the white middle-class model.

Leeds, Olly. "The Separatists' Fantasy." <u>Liberator</u> 9 (February 1969): 4-7.

The author advocates self-help (myth-making and skill-building) to prepare the black masses for liberation and points out the practical shortcomings of separatists' demands for an independent state.

Lester, Julius. "The Necessity for Separation." <u>Ebony</u> 25 (August 1970): 167-69.

American history has demonstrated the futility of integration. Only in a black nation will black people be regarded as human beings. Nevertheless, a black nation will not automatically solve all problems. Many existing problems will continue, and new ones will be created.

Lightfoot, Claude. "The Right of Black America to Create a Black Nation." Political Affairs 47 (November 1968): 1-11.*

Lincoln, C. Eric. My Face Is Black. Boston: Beacon, 1964.

The black power movement is a response to the white racist back-lash to the civil rights movement. Many blacks have an "Armageddon complex," which causes them to become cynical about the possibility of integration and to expect a racial conflagration.

Llorens, David. "Black Separatism in Perspective: Movement Reflects Failure of Integration." Ebony 23 (September 1968): 88-95.

The Republic of New Africa was founded in Detroit in 1968. Llorens relates it to earlier forms of territorial separatism and to the failure of the civil rights movement. The ideas of the founding officers of RNA are described. Their tactics include a plebiscite in black communities on separatism and formation of a Black Legion to train members for an eventual forceful takeover of the five Deep South states.

Mack, Raymond W. "The Negro Opposition to Black Extremism." Saturday Review 51 (May 4, 1968): 52-55.

A nationwide attitudinal survey which indicated that nowhere in the country did most black Americans subscribe to separatism or prefer black schools for black children.

McKissick, Floyd. Three-Fifths of a Man. New York: Macmillan, 1969.

The Constitution and the doctrine of black nationalism are two complementary instruments that could save America. Nationalism is not extremist; rather it means a commitment and sense of responsibility to one's own kind. McKissick suggests that the black community should be provided with the resources to solve its own problems. He estimates that only ten percent of black Americans are interested in integration, and that the proportion would drop further if feasible alternatives were available.

Malcolm X and Farmer, James. "Separation or Integration: A Debate." Dialogue Magazine 2 (May 1962): 14-18.

James Farmer, in support of integration, cites CORE's program and the work of other civil rights organizations to further equality for blacks. Malcolm X asserts that separation is the only answer to the racial problems in the United States and proposes the creation of a black state.

Mboya, Tom. "The American Negro Cannot Look to Africa for an Escape." <u>New York Times</u>, 13 July 1969, pp. 30-31+.

During a speech at the Countee Cullen Branch Library in New York, March 1969, Mboya opposed mass movement of black Americans back to Africa and urged them not to desist from the struggle for equality because of impatience with progress. Here, Mboya expands on this theme of black African/black American relations, reiterating the need for mutual support. He affirms the greater need for black Americans not to diffuse energy and emotion, goals and priorities into debates which would splinter a free and vigorous black community. Rather, he hopes for a unified black leadership which would be more instrumental in meeting the challenges in this country and more effective in helping newly emerging African nations.

Menard, Orville D. "America's Emerging Nation." <u>Midwest Quarterly</u> 12 (January 1971): 137-44.

Self-determinism is a more tangible goal than integration.

Merton, Robert K. "Insiders and Outsiders: A Chapter in the Sociology of Knowledge." <u>American Journal of Sociology</u> 78 (July 1972): 46-66.

A theoretical discussion of the claim of militant black intellectuals that only black intellectuals can understand black culture. Who can better analyze a social system, the Insider or Outsider? The author presents a case for both and concludes that only a merger of the two can overcome the bias of the Insider and the lack of sensitivity of the Outsider.

Morsell, John A. "Futility of Black Self-Segregation." <u>New York Times</u>, 7 March 1968, p. 42.

In a letter to the editor, Morsell condemns the racism inherent in black self-segregation and "skin-deep liberalism" that withers in the face of black extremists' rejection, anger, and accusations. Black self-segregation is not attainable in this country; whites who support it are simply easing their consciences because they are only tenuously committed to the ideal of racial equality in an integrated society.

National Advisory Commission on Civil Disorders. Report. New York: Bantam, 1968.

The President's Advisory Commission, appointed after the 1964 Watts riot, warns that America is headed toward two separate and unequal nations—black and white. The report describes the ghetto riots of the 1960s, analyzes why they happened, and makes recommendations.

"The Negro and American Values, A Conversation Between James Farmer and Algernon D. Black." Humanist 28 (March-April 1968): 7-9.

The integration-separation issue is an academic one for the black masses; the middle class is primarily interested in integration. Farmer sees validity in both the need for integration and the need for group cohesiveness which grows out of a common racial and cultural background.

Newman, Richard. "The American Racial Crisis." Contemporary Review 213 (September 1968): 121-24, 145.

Black power is defined as a bridge between the old civil rights movement and black nationalism, which militants feel will mean equality for the masses of blacks. The tenets of black nationalism; the notions of separatism, racial awareness, and pride are also discussed.

"Now It's a Negro Drive for Segregation." U.S. News and World Report 56 (March 30, 1964): 38-39.

Interview with Malcolm X and a discussion of the Black Muslim program of black nationalism. Malcolm states that the integration movement has resulted only in further segregation. The immediate solution is to improve separate facilities; the ultimate solution is to return to Africa.

Obadele, Imari Abubakari. "Come to the Land." Rhythm 1 (Fall 1970): 26-29.

A declaration and rationale for the creation of a black nation out of five states: Louisiana, Mississippi, Alabama, Georgia, and South Carolina. Current developments, for example, acquisition of land in Mississippi and building activity, are described.

Obadele, Imari Abubakari. "Republic of New Africa: The Struggle for Land in Mississippi." Black World 22 (February 1973): 66-73.

The president of the Republic of New Africa estimates that five million blacks would repatriate to a black nation in the South.

Their emigration would increase the social services available to those remaining in the inner cities; thus, separation would benefit those who choose to remain in the pluralistic society. Obadele analyzes the response of the American judicial system and the press to the behavior of black nationalists.

Obadele, Imari Abubakari. <u>Revolution and Nation Building</u>. Detroit: House of Songhay, 1970.

A manual on how to create an independent black state in the United States.

O'Dell, John H. "The Contours of the 'Black Revolution' in the 1970s." <u>Freedomways</u> 10 (Second Quarter 1970): 104-14.

The Freedom Movement of the 1960s used mass direct action as the primary instrument of social emancipation for blacks. In the 1970s these strategies will develop into a revolution involving a cross section of ethnic groups and socioeconomic classes. This revolution will not be an isolated "Black Revolution."

Ohmann, Carol. "The Autobiography of Malcolm X: A Revolutionary Use of the Franklin Tradition." <u>American Quarterly</u> 22 (Summer 1970): 131-49.

A comparison of the autobiographies of Malcolm X and Benjamin Franklin which analyzes their very distinct differences but also points out how they resemble each other in the conceptions of self and in the standards by which they perceive and judge men and events. This author argues that in the last chapters of his auto-biography, Malcolm X does not present the dominant image of a black militant. Rather, he is a man convinced of the need for the creation of a society in which honest black-white brotherhood could exist.

Parenti, Michael. "Assimilation and Counter-Assimilation: From Civil Rights to Black Radicalism." In <u>Power and Community</u>, edited by Philip Green and Sanford Lewis, pp. 172-94. New York: Pantheon, 1970.

The view that, with more time and more education, blacks will assimilate into American culture and social structure is based on an outdated and incorrect assimilationist ideology which fails to realize that other minority groups did not really assimilate. The movement toward black power and black identity stems from this realization heightened by the further realization that the black man has not followed, but rather been a victim of, the immigrant experience. Black radicalism goes one step further to state that inequities can only be remedied by total economic and social change away from a class-privileged capitalist system.

Patterson, Orlando. "Rethinking Black History." Harvard Educational Review 41 (August 1971): 297-315.

An analysis and critical assessment of contemporary interpretations of black history: radical and conservative catastrophism, radical and conservative survivalism, and contributionism. The author makes a case for different theoretical and methodological approaches to the subject through the use of alternative methods of historical inquiry as well as oral, nonwritten and nonliterary, sources.

"Penthouse Interview/ Roy Innis, Black Nationalist," with Mark Monsky. Penthouse (January 1970): 28-32.

Innis defines black nationalism as a locale (wherever black people live), as an ideal (blacks should control their own social and political institutions), and as a developing program to offer solutions to the problems of the black masses.

Pettigrew, Thomas F. Racially Separate or Together? New York: McGraw-Hill, 1971.

Pettigrew contends that integration is the only way to eradicate white racism. Part One examines institutional racism in the urban context. Part Two examines the role of the social sciences in understanding and combating racism at both the institutional and individual levels. Part Three extends this type of social-psychological analysis to trends since World War II in racial attidues of both black and white Americans. Part Four discusses the constituencies of two antiblack politicians. Part Five considers the argument that integration is a societal imperative.

Piven, Frances Fox, and Cloward, Richard A. "What Chance for Black Power?" New Republic 158 (March 30, 1968): 19-23.

Suggests that integrated institutions serve white interests and, therefore, blacks must develop separate institutions to acquire power.

"Playboy Interviews: Malcolm X." In Playboy Interviews, pp. 33-51. Chicago: Playboy Press, 1969.

Interviewed by Alex Haley early in 1963, Malcolm X asserts that blacks are superior to whites, and discusses the need for separation of the races. He also analyzes the function of black civic leaders and the character of the white man.

Powell, Adam Clayton, Jr. "Can There Any Good Thing Come Out of Nazareth?" Baccalaureate Address, Howard University, May 29, 1966, Washington, D. C.

A call for blacks to seek "audacious power—more black power" to build black institutions rather than to seek integration.

Record, Wilson. "American Racial Ideologies and Organizations in Transition." Phylon 26 (Winter 1965): 315-29.

An analysis of the programs and ideologies of the most prominent black protest organizations, NAACP, SNCC, CORE, SCLC. The author believes that the political left and right have not influenced or threatened these groups. Reference is made to the separatist movement of the Black Muslims and to self-help projects.

Record, Wilson. "Extremist Movements Among American Negroes." Phylon 17 (First Quarter 1956): 17-23.

Black extremist movements seek to withdraw the black population from society as a whole or to change society in some fundamental way, rather than to integrate blacks into the social order as it exists. Record thinks that black extremism has been largely ignored and suggests several methodologies for studying it.

Robeson, Paul. Here I Stand. New York: McClelland, 1958.

In these autobiographical essays Robeson describes his personal philosophy. He believes that white Americans will support blacks in their quest for equal rights and that organized labor occupies the key position in the civil rights movement because labor has the opportunity to rally white unionists to the support of equal rights. He also discusses the development of his political views as a result of his visits to Africa and the Soviet Union.

Rustin, Bayard. Down the Line, the Collected Writings of Bayard Rustin. Chicago: Quadrangle, 1971.

In this collection of writings drawn from newspaper columns, magazine articles, speeches, and pamphlets, Rustin speaks about his active concern for oppressed minorities, especially blacks. His cyclical theory of black history—repeated and contrary movements of violence, withdrawal, separatism, and nationalism—forms the rationale for his goals for blacks: civil rights, equality, and integration; and his strategies for achieving these goals: the ballot, union membership, and coalition politics.

Rustin, Bayard. "The Failure of Black Separatism." Harper's 240 (January 1970): 25-32.

A critical review of the separatist movement in labor, economics, and education. Rustin states that the call for community control by black power advocates in "an adjustment to inequality rather than a protest against it." Many students use black studies for political and ideological reasons rather than as an educational endeavor designed to explore the contribution of blacks to the American experience.

Safa, Helen Icken. "The Case for Negro Separatism." Urban Affairs Quarterly 4 (September 1968): 45-63. *

Schrag, Peter. "The New Black Myths." Harper's 238 (May 1969): 37-42.

Schrag explores the paradoxes of the black experience in America. He thinks that black nationalism—puritanical, messianic, and bourgeois—is simply the prevailing American myth colored black. In coming to terms with the problems exemplified by the rhetoric of black power, our society will become more humane.

Sherrill, Robert. "Whitey's Reaction to Proposal of Separate Black State." Esquire 71 (January 1969): 76-77+.

Discusses the practical and impractical sides of the separate black state movement and includes quotations from southern politicians.

Sinnette, Calvin H. "Repatriation—Dead Issue or Resurrected Alternative?" Freedomways 8 (Winter 1968): 57-63.

Afro-Americans are a surplus population and their survival and liberation in America is endangered; therefore, blacks should seriously consider a planned and logically graduated program of voluntary repatriation to Africa.

Smith, Bob. "The Case Against Blackthink." Virginia Quarterly Review 44 (Winter 1968): 43-50.

The chronic "blackthink" of civil rights professionals has led to a racism similar to the one fled. Blacks' problems are predominantly problems of the poor and problems of the city, and laws such as open-housing, designed to end racial segregation but not bad plumbing, will not solve these problems.

Storing, Herbert J., ed. What Country Have I? New York: St. Martin's, 1970.

A collection of essays discussing political directions of blacks. The authors variously favor political integration, political separation, and spatial separation. Some of the writers included are

W. E. B. DuBois, Malcolm X, Stokely Carmichael, Charles Hamilton, Eldridge Cleaver, and Albert B. Cleage, Jr.

"Support Builds for RNA Eleven; RNA Fact Sheet." CORE 2 (February/ March 1972): 59-66.

A fact sheet showing the organizational activities and legal problems of the Republic of New Africa.

"Talk Up Racism." New Republic 159 (July 20, 1968): 9-10.

In 1968 it appeared that black leaders were under irresistible pressure from their constituents to talk the language of black independence, if not black separatism. When the rhetoric is tuned out, it appears that what is advocated is not as radical as is often hinted. Speaking at the 1968 CORE convention, Roy Wilkins and Whitney Young dismissed the idea of geographical separation (a convention vote agreed with them) but emphasized the validity of self-determination and community control.

Thomas, Tony, ed. Black Liberation and Socialism. New York: Pathfinder Press, 1974.

A collection of articles in the revolutionary socialist tradition of Marx, Lenin, and Trotsky as a tool for the black liberation struggle.

Tinker, Irene. "Nationalism in a Plural Society: The Case of the American Negro." Western Political Quarterly 19 (March 1966): 112-22.

The growth of black nationalism and its dangers for American society reflect the critical problem of any unassimilated minority in a plural society. Pressures toward militancy are difficult to resist if accommodation is not forthcoming. Some accommodation for guaranteed minority representation may help to mitigate the trend toward militancy are difficult to resist if accommodation is not forthcoming. Some accommodation for guaranteed minority representation may help to mitigate the trend toward militancy in the black movement.

Tucker, Sterling. "Black Strategies for Change in America." Journal of Negro Education 40 (Summer 1970): 297-311.

Neither integration nor separatism is a goal in itself; both can result in poverty and powerlessness. Tucker distinguishes between the value of a sense of separate identity and the destructiveness of organizing oneself out of society. Existing separate institutions

such as ghetto schools and housing must be upgraded into effectiveness, but such efforts must not lead to a belief that a separate society is possible.

Turner, James. "Black Nationalism: The Inevitable Response." Black
World 20 (January 1971): 3-13.

Black nationalism is the inevitable response to the failure of integration as a strategy and goal for black Americans. The author
defines black nationalism as a multifaceted technique for survival
and philosophy of reality that addresses itself to the racial question
and to the creation of a corporate self-awareness and unity among
black Americans.

Vincent, Theodore G. Black Power and the Garvey Movement.
Berkeley: Ramparts Press, 1971.

In his reinterpretation of standard studies of Garvey, Vincent asserts that Garvey constructed the ideological basis for modern
black nationalism. This, not the financial and organizational failure of the UNIA, is the significant aspect of Garveyism. Vincent
disputes Cronon's point that Garveyism was primarily a back-to-
Africa movement. Garvey intended to send only a few hundred
thousand American blacks to Africa to strengthen ties between
blacks in the U.S. and Africa. In calling for the development of a
separate society, Garvey referred to separate institutions, not
territorial separation. His business enterprise program was consistent with Booker T. Washington's ideas, but his support of
capitalism was based essentially on a refusal to cooperate with the
white-dominated socialist movement rather than on a belief in the
validity of the capitalist economy.

Vivian, C. T. Black Power and the American Myth. Philadelphia:
Fortress Press, 1970.

Genuine integration will never work for blacks because whites hold
the power for its success. Separatism is the response of black
people to the failure of integration. The new movement is taking
such forms as black caucuses, community control of schools, and
awareness of an identity with black culture.

Ward, Hiley H. Prophet of the Black Nation. Philadelphia: Pilgrim
Press, 1969.

Chapter 2 of this biography of Reverend Albert B. Cleage, Jr.,
describes his particular form of nationalism—a program based on
black consciousness, black pride, unity, and the principle of self-
determination to develop a "nation within a nation."

Warren, Robert Penn. "Malcolm X: Mission and Meaning. " <u>Yale Review</u> 56 (Winter 1967): 161-71.

When Malcolm X was killed, he was still searching for a philosophy. Having partially rejected the separatist doctrines of the Muslims, he was ready to work with other black organizations for a "bloodless revolution." He never gave up his philosophy of race pride, personal self-respect and self-improvement, or his rage and radical indictment of white society.

Weiss, Samuel A. "The Ordeal of Malcolm X. " <u>South Atlantic Quarterly</u> 67 (Winter 1968): 53-63.

Weiss thinks that Malcolm's world-view and prophesies were accurate, and that American society must be changed in the ways Malcolm visualized. His influence on blacks during his lifetime will be exceeded by his importance after his death.

"What's Happening to America?" <u>Urban Crisis Monitor</u> (August 5, 1968): 12-13.

In a wide-ranging discussion of race problems in America, Kenneth B. Clark and C. Vann Woodward touch on black separatism. White and black separatism share the same psychological basis, a superstition of race and color. Black separatism may further the dialogue on racism; whites will see racist arguments more clearly when they come from blacks, and may understand the inherent irrationality.

Wilkins, Roy. "Integration. " <u>Ebony</u> 25 (August 1970): 54-59.

In a rigorous argument against separatism, the author points out the failures of separatist movements since the first serious emigration efforts began about 1714. Wilkins favors instead a dependence on the long, slow, difficult but successful integration strategy.

Wilson, James A. "White Power and Black Supremacy. " <u>Pittsburgh Business Review</u> 37 (August 1967): 12-14.

Black separatism, as a response to segregation, is morally justified except when it results in hostility toward whites.

Woodmansee, John J., and Rucker, Richard. "A Scale of Black Separatism. " <u>Psychological Reports</u> 27 (December 1970): 855-58.

A study based on responses of 257 black students to questions designed to measure their receptivity to five organizations, The Urban League, NAACP, SCLC, CORE, SNCC, and the Black Panther Party. Only strong responses in favor of the Black Panther Party could be differentiated.

Wormley, Stanton L., and Fenderson, Lewis H., eds. Many Shades of Black. New York: William Morrow, 1969.

    A collection of essays by eminent black men and women in the fields of civil rights and social action, the arts, science, business, sports, foreign affairs, and the ministry. Among the contributors are Franklin H. Williams and William H. Hastie who express faith in a society and government hesitant to share justice and equality with black Americans. They see a reshaping of the social order through blacks' persistent efforts at group and self-improvement and marshaling of intelligence and skills to achieve equality through the legal process.

Wright, Nathan. "The Crisis Which Bred Black Power." In The Black Power Revolt, edited by Floyd B. Barbour, pp. 117-35. New York: Collier, 1968.

    Integration has clearly failed; there can be no meaningful integration between unequals. Blacks need solidarity if they are to achieve self-sufficiency. Whites can facilitate black power by removing specific barriers in education and employment.

Young, Whitney M., Jr. Beyond Racism: Building an Open Society. New York: McGraw-Hill, 1969.

    This examination of racism in contemporary America includes a brief section describing black power as the goal of integration. Young does not think that separatism will work as a means of gaining black power.

Young, Whitney M., Jr. "Separatism? We Are Separated—and That's the Cause of All Our Woes." Ebony 25 (August 1970): 90-96.

    The author asserts his belief in the need for an integrated society. Integration, however, need not entail a loss of a sense of blackness.

Part Two: Institutional and Psychological Dimensions

3. IDENTITY: INDIVIDUAL AND COLLECTIVE

Baldwin, James. "Many Thousands Gone." In Notes of a Native Son, pp. 24-25. Boston: Beacon, 1955.

First published in Partisan Review in 1951, this essay shows Baldwin attempting to evaluate the black person's place in American society. "Negroes are Americans and their destiny is the country's destiny. They have no experience besides their experience on this continent and it is experience which cannot be rejected, which yet remains to be embraced." Baldwin discusses the limit of the symbolic validity of Bigger Thomas, the protagonist in Richard Wright's Native Son.

Baraka, Imamu Amiri. Blues People; Negro Music in White America. New York: William Morrow, 1963.

Music represents in microcosm the process of Americanization of Africans. It is the one element peculiar to blacks in both slavery and freedom, and both symbolizes and delineates the stages of change involved in the transition. Development of the blues marks the appearance of American blacks as a conscious group.

Baraka, Imamu Amiri. Raise Race Rays Raze: Essays Since 1965. New York: Vintage, 1971. *

Bennett, Lerone, Jr. "What's in a Name? Negro vs. Afro-American vs. Black." Ebony 23 (November 1967): 46-50.

A historical sketch of the word "Negro" as an accepted term by the Negro community as well as a discussion of the continuous and sustained opposition to the term.

"Black English: Route or Roadblock to Racial Progress?" Race Relations and Industry 9 (February 1974): 1-4.

Discusses an experiment which shows that dialect significantly affects verbal test scores. The research cited indicates that rejection and condemnation of black language tend to have negative results in student attitudes, while the teaching of Standard English as an alternative mode of speech might result in more rapid student progress.

"Black Nonsense. " Crisis 78 (April-May 1971): 78.

This editorial warns black parents that the use of black English in the instruction of black children amounts to an "insidious conspiracy to cripple their children permanently" because basic English is the language of science, technology, and national power.

Bone, Robert A. The Negro Novel in America. New Haven: Yale University Press, 1958.

The group experience marks the distinction between black and white writers. Antiwhite sentiment provides the psychological impetus for black nationalism, which leads to racial solidarity and pride. The concepts of assimilationism and nationalism are used to interpret the work of black novelists, and to gauge the temper of periods.

Brawley, Benjamin. The Negro Genius. New York: Dodd, Mead, 1937. Reprint. New York: Biblo and Tannen, 1966.

In the introduction to this historical survey of culture and the arts produced by black Americans, Brawley asserts that only blacks with little or no white blood are capable of artistic genius. Brawley includes a chapter on protest leaders who represent what he calls "Negro genius"—men such as W. E. B. DuBois, James Weldon Johnson, and Walter White.

Browne, Robert S. "The Challenge of Black Student Organizations. " Freedomways 8 (Fall 1968): 325-33. *

Brown, Robert S. , and Rustin, Bayard. Separatism or Integration: Which Way for America? New York: A. Philip Randolph Institute, 1968. *

Butcher, Margaret Just. The Negro in American Culture. New York: Knopf, 1956.

Based on material left at the death of Alain Locke, this monograph covers various art forms. Butcher asserts that blacks have been slow to achieve eminence in formal and sophisticated fields (for example, fiction, literary and art criticism) as a result of their exclusion from educational opportunities. The black experience has greatly influenced the way in which black artists have used media, but folk culture and Africanisms have been less important than mainstream art movement.

Cade, Toni, ed. The Black Woman; An Anthology. New York: New American Library, 1970.

The preface to this anthology of black women's writings states that sexual as well as racial stereotypes limit the black woman's potential. Many black women have formed discussion groups and task forces to define and rework the factors influencing their lives.

Caliguri, Joseph P. "Black Power and Black Students in Kansas City." Integrated Education 10 (January-February 1972): 41-48.*

Carmichael, Stokely. "Power and Racism: What We Want." New York Review of Books (September 22, 1966): 5-8.

"Black power" is defined as a strategy to obtain political power for blacks in proportion to their numbers, as well as economic self-determination based on cooperative socialism. Integration as a goal is criticized because it is based on acceptance of white institutions as superior and therefore the ideal. Integration would be acceptable if it meant white acceptance of black institutions.

"CBE Interviews: Kenneth B. Clark." Council for Basic Education Bulletin 14 (November 1969): 8-18.

Interviewed by Dante Peter Ciochetto, Clark answers questions about the education of minority-group children. He argues against the acceptance of black dialect in the schools on an equal basis with Standard English because students will need Standard English to compete in society.

Chisholm, Shirley. "Race, Revolution and Women." Black Scholar 3 (December 1971): 17-21.

Racial and sexual discrimination have forced males and females as well as blacks and whites to operate separately to avoid conflict. Chisholm thinks that society must strive for the integration of male and female, as well as white and black.

Chisholm, Shirley. "Racism and Anti-Feminism." Black Scholar 1 (January-February 1970): 40-45.

The roots and goals of antifeminism and racism are synonymous. Chisholm thinks that all discrimination is simply reducible to antihumanism.

Chrisman, Robert. "Formation of a Revolutionary Black Culture." Black Scholar 1 (June 1970): 2-9.

White America has divided blacks by racism and classism. If blacks seriously want to develop a revolutionary black nationalism, they must understand these divisions and attack them simultaneously by analysis of class-race divisions in the black community; by meshing all black organizations; and by furthering black culture in the arts, in psychology, and in educational propaganda.

Clark, Kenneth B. "The Dangerous Inefficiency of Racially Separated Schools." In Integration and Separatism in Education, edited by Samuel Goldman and Peter L. Clark, pp. 9-18. Syracuse: Syracuse University Press, 1970. *

Clark, Kenneth B. "The Failure: Three Experts Discuss It, and What Could Be Done." South Today 2 (December 1970): 4, 10.

Excerpt from testimony before the Senate Select Committee on Equal Educational Opportunity. Clark testifies in favor of busing for integration, and analyzes the effect of prejudice and segregation on white youth. He interprets separatism as a sympton of the unfulfilled promise of integration.

Clark, Kenneth B. "The Social Scientists, the Brown Decision, and Contemporary Confusion." In Argument: The Oral Argument Before the Supreme Court in Brown v. Board of Education of Topeka 1952-55, edited by Leon Friedman, pp. xxxi-1. New York: Chelsea House, 1969.

Clark observes that black nationalism has adopted an imitation of white racism under the guise of assuming a positive identity. The quest for identity is based on superstition, since the conditions of inequality remain. Separatism is basically an attempt to create verbal realities as substitutes for social, political, and economic realities. Black racists, as well as white racists, are people who have given up on their capacity to advance justice.

Clarke, John Henrik. "The New Afro-American Nationalism." Freedomways 1 (Fall 1961): 285-95.

Concerned with the attempt of black Americans to reclaim their African heritage, this essay emphasizes the new nationalism's basis in religions and customs that originated in Africa. Clarke thinks that cultural components are a more important aspect of the new nationalism than emigration.

Cleage, Albert B., Jr. "Black Power—An Advocate Defines It." Public Relations Journal 24 (July 1968): 17-18.

Black power means self-determination for the black community. It means the creation of a black cultural nation based on a common heritage and common oppression, not a geographic or political unit.

Cole, Johnnetta B. "Culture: Negro, Black and Nigger." Black Scholar 1 (June 1970): 40-44.

The black subculture combines a mainstream American materialism with a detector for bigotry and soul. This article deals with soul, its identifiability and its manifestations in life styles.

Conference of Negro Writers. The American Negro Writer and His
Roots: Selected Papers. New York: American Society of African
Culture, 1960.

> Includes papers by J. Saunders Redding, John Henrik Clarke,
> Langston Hughes, and others. Arthur P. Davis writes that inte-
> gration has transformed and will continue to transform black liter-
> ature. Protest writing went out of date shortly after the civil rights
> movement became a part of the national consciousness, but racial
> strife has kept black writing focused on narrow social issues,
> rather than on universal human concerns.

Cooke, Anne. "Black Pride? Some Contradictions." Negro Digest
19 (January 1970): 36-42+.

> Cooke analyzes certain trends relating to black awareness, in-
> cluding the misuses of African languages and dress, the adoption
> of Islam, and the tendency to break away from white culture and
> organizations only to parallel them with white-allowed culture for
> blacks. She recommends the development of black culture.

Coombs, Orde. "The Death and Life of Malcolm X." New York
Times, 28 January 1973, p. 40.

> In this review of The Death and Life of Malcolm X by Peter Gold-
> man, Coombs states that black writing should be criticized and
> evaluated by whites as well as blacks; if a work has any appeal
> and value, its worth is universal. Whites who refuse to make
> critical judgments about writing by blacks are avoiding a moral
> responsibility.

Cummings, Gwenna. "Black Women—Often Discussed but Never Understood." In The Black Power Revolt, edited by Floyd B.
Barbour, pp. 281-86. New York: Collier, 1968.

> The social role of black women is even more complex than that of
> black men because racial discrimination is compounded by sexual
> discrimination. Cummings thinks that black women have devel-
> oped special strengths that enable them to fill a leadership role in
> the family when men are not present.

Cunningham, James. "Ron Karenga and Black Cultural Nationalism."
Negro Digest 17 (January 1968): 4, 76-80.

> A criticism of Ron Karenga's cultural nationalism. Cunningham
> particularly attacks Karenga's idea that blacks must be force-fed
> a wholly black culture as unrealistic and paternalistic.

Davis, Angela. "Reflections on the Black Woman's Role in the Community of Slaves." Black Scholar 3 (December 1971): 3-15.*

Dillard, J. L. Black English; Its History and Usage in the United States. New York: Random House, 1972.

This study investigates the historical and grammatical origins of black English; stressing the view that as an operative tongue, it is not a misuse of Standard English but a precise language of its own. As such, it has a positive role to play in the education of children using it, particularly if teachers understand its relevance in communicating with ghetto children and use it as an approach to teaching Standard English.

Dover, Cedric. American Negro Art. New York: New York Graphic Society, 1960.

Primarily a collection of reproductions of paintings, sculpture, and other visual art forms. The compiler includes an introductory essay in which he states that although black artists produce fully American art, contemporary black artists should continue to remain a minority school within the broader art world.

DuBois, W. E. B. "Jim Crow." Crisis 17 (January 1919): 112-13.*

DuBois, W. E. B. "On Being Ashamed of Oneself, an Essay on Race Pride." Crisis 40 (September 1933): 199-200.

DuBois calls for a new black attitude of race pride to support the crusade to strengthen black institutions. Blacks will have to make their own segregated institutions viable becasue "there seems no hope that America in our day will yield in its color or race hatred any substantial ground and we have no physical nor economic power nor any alliance with other social or economic classes that will force compliance with decent civilized ideals in church, state, industry or art."

DuBois, W. E. B. "Our Book Shelf." Crisis 31 (January 1926): 141.

In this review of The New Negro, edited by Alain Locke, DuBois reaffirms his belief in the use of art as propaganda, and his expectation that the black artist's role is primarily to serve the race, to uplift. "This is a book filled with propaganda for the most part beautifully and painstakingly done; and it is a grave question if ever in this world in any renaissance there can be a search for disembodied beauty which is not really a passionate effort to do something tangible, accompanied and illumined and made holy by the vision of eternal beauty."

Durley, Gerald L. "A Center for Black Students on University Campuses." Journal of Higher Education 40 (June 1969): 473-76. *

Essien-Udom, E. U. Black Nationalism: The Search for an Identity in America. Chicago: University of Chicago Press, 1962.

The Nigerian-born author writes in his preface: "This book is about the phenomenon of black nationalism in the United States—the effort of thousands of American Negroes to resolve for themselves this fundamental problem of identity and to provide a context for their moral, cultural, and material advancement within the limits set by the American scene." The book describes the ideology of black nationalism—its organization, leaders, and programs, focusing on the Nation of Islam.

Frazier, E. Franklin. The Negro in the United States. New York: Macmillan, 1949.

This study examines the trend toward integration, which Frazier sees as desirable and inevitable. Integration is occurring first in areas of life that involve secondary rather than primary contacts; thus, integration in schools and jobs is more easily attained than in private relations. Integration in American society is occurring in part because of increased internationalism since World War II.

Gaffney, Floyd. "Black Theatre: Commitment and Communication." Black Scholar 1 (June 1970): 10-15.

Black playwrights belong to the black community, but only if they rely on their experience will their works relate to that community. It is the obligation of the playwrights to persevere against lack of funding and weak criticism.

Garland X. "Black Women Turn from 'Feminism.'" Muhammad Speaks, 29 June 1973, p. 27.

A report on the National Black Women's Political Leadership Caucus Convention held in Washington, D. C., on June 1, 1973. The consensus was that there is a need for more aggressive political behavior for black women with no need for participation in the white feminist movement.

Hare, Nathan. "How White Power Whitewashes Black Power." In The Black Power Revolt, edited by Floyd B. Barbour, pp. 215-24. New York: Collier, 1968.

Black power is a nonracist response to the pervasiveness of white power and to the failure of assimilation. Instead of showing concern about the white backlash, Hare thinks that blacks should prepare to clash with white oppression.

Hare, Nathan. "Rebels Without a Name." Phylon 23 (Fall 1962): 271-77.

  An analysis of the historical processes of the effort to abolish the name Negro, to define the name, and to find a new name.

Harris, William H. "The Militant Separatists in the White Academy." American Scholar 41 (Summer 1972): 366-76.

  A discussion of the increased importance of separatism to black students. The main effect of separatism has been to shift the emphasis of the black movement from freedom to identity. Identity is a main concern to both black and white youth; separatism provides a basis for blacks' identity which integration does not provide.

Hastie, William H. "The Black Mystique Pitfall." Crisis 78 (October 1971): 243-47.

  Although much remains to be done, the persistent activities of the NAACP over the last thirty years have succeeded in outlawing segregation in American life. However, during the 1960s, the number of blacks who accepted and encouraged racial separatism increased dramatically, and now many blacks, particularly the youth, are arguing and practicing a self-inflicted segregation and glorifying their blackness to compensate for other shortcomings. This "racial mystique" is as harmful to blacks as it is to whites.

Hill, Adelaide Cromwell. "What Is Africa to Us?" In The Black Power Revolt, edited by Floyd B. Barbour, pp. 145-55. New York: Colher, 1968.

  In this paper delivered at the 1967 National Conference on Black Power, held in Newark, New Jersey, Hill suggests that blacks are developing a new self-concept based on identification with Africa and knowledge of African cultures. This new attitude will yield increased self-pride among young blacks giving them the strength to achieve personal goals and social change.

Jordan, June. "Black English: The Politics of Translation." Library Journal 98 (May 15, 1973): 163-64.

  The denigration of black language represents a deliberate display of power intended to destroy the powerless. Acquisition of Standard English is necessary for self-preservation, but it should remain secondary to the black language which embodies the spirit, culture, and experience of black people and is necessary for continued survival.

Jordan, June. "White English: The Politics of Language." Black World 22 (August 1973): 4-10.

Blacks and whites must acknowledge black English not as a substandard variety of white English or Standard English, but as a legitimate language to be formally taught in the regular school curriculum.

Keil, Charles. Urban Blues. Chicago: University of Chicago Press, 1966.

An analysis of black music, particularly urban blues, in terms of its cultural values. Study of black music provides an opportunity for the study of cultural diffusion, acculturation, and syncretism; Keil finds strong evidences of African heritage. The demands for cultural pluralism symbolized by the revitalization of black music will help blacks avoid assimilation and the obliteration of black culture.

Killens, John O. "The Artist in the Black University." Black Scholar 1 (November 1969): 61-65.

As the emphasis of the civil rights movement changed from integration to black consciousness, artists began to assume important roles. The ensuing cultural revolution on campus was reflected in demands for black universities and for black studies programs in white universities. Killens supports the idea of a "black communiversity" to provide an opportunity for black artists, scholars, teachers, activists, and students to meet and learn from one another. For those students who attend predominantly white colleges, black studies programs facilitate the development of a positive racial identity. The academic standards for black studies programs should be high; the militant student should be the best student.

King, Helen. "The Black Woman and Women's Lib." Ebony 26 (March 1971): 68-76.

The consensus from blacks on women's liberation is that black women should identify with the black liberation struggle rather than with feminism.

Labov, William. <u>Language in the Inner City: Studies in the Black English Vernacular.</u> Philadelphia: University of Pennsylvania Press, 1972.

A study of the uniform dialect spoken by the majority of black youth from eight to nineteen years of age especially in the inner city areas of large cities to assess its impact on reading failure. The major causes of reading problems are political and cultural conflicts in the classroom in which language differences are an important factor.

Ladner, Joyce A. <u>Tomorrow's Tomorrow: The Black Woman.</u> Garden City, N.Y.: Doubleday, 1971.

A separate black culture exists, comprised of Africanisms and adaptive responses to slavery and discrimination. The dualism resulting from conflicting values of the white and black cultures is strongly reflected in the lives of black women. Black culture and society should be protected and strengthened to ease the psychological stresses, which fall particularly heavily on black women.

LaRue, Linda. "The Black Movement and Women's Liberation." <u>Black Scholar</u> 1 (May 1970): 36-42.

The author disagrees with the frequent linking of the oppression of women with the oppression of blacks. She sees the need for role integration—that is, complementing and harmonizing the strengths of men and women in their roles as citizens and companions.

Lewis, Hylan. "Changing Aspiration, Images and Identities." In <u>The Educationally Deprived: The Potential for Change,</u> by Kenneth B. Clark, et al., pp. 30-46. New York: Metropolitan Applied Research Center, 1972.

The problem of making ghetto schools responsive to the changing aspirations and self-concept of minority students and parents is tied to the larger political situation. New formulas for eliminating inequities in education (as well as in housing, health, and welfare) are tied to concepts of black power, which increase the difficulty of the white power structure to come to terms with valid demands.

Lincoln, C. Eric. "How Negroes Rediscovered Their Racial Pride." <u>Negro Digest</u> 10 (July 1961): 71-76.

Blacks' long struggle for acceptance as human beings and the emergence of the newly independent African states are two reasons for the new appreciation of blackness. This mood of self-confidence and spirit of protest undergirds a range of activities from participation in black-oriented, white-rejecting groups such as the Black Muslims, Ras Tafarians, and Women of African Heritage, to nonviolent sit-ins and passive resistance.

Longino, Charles F. , and Wagoner, Jennings L. "Educational Criticism and the Transformation of Black Consciousness." Educational Forum 36 (May 1972): 499-506.

Black power must be understood in social-psychological terms to be fully appreciated. Black power is fundamentally a problem of consciousness; the demands blacks are making on public education are manifestations of the phenomenon.

McClintock, Ernie. "Perspective on Black Acting." Black World 23 (May 1974): 79-85.

For the black actor and audience, drama should provide a spiritually uplifting and reflective experience which leads to conscious or unconscious positive actions. McClintock, director of the Afro-American Studio for Acting and Speech, describes the Harlem school's program. His method, "common-sense technique," emphasizes the need for the actor's skill and imagination to create believable illuminations of each character portrayed.

McConnell, Frank D. "Black Words and Black Becoming." Yale Review 63 (Winter 1974): 193-210.

McConnell concerns himself with identity in the works of several black writers, from Frederick Douglass to Eldridge Cleaver. These writers were dealing with the most important aspect of the black revolution, the nonmaterial needs of the black community, identity and consciousness.

Malcolm X. The Autobiography of Malcolm X with the assistance of Alex Haley. New York: Grove, 1965.

This book, put together from tape-recorded conversations, is the record of Malcolm's agonizing search for identity.

Margolies, Edward. Native Sons: A Critical Study of Twentieth-Century Negro American Authors. Philadelphia: Lippincott, 1968.

An analysis of the work of major twentieth-century black writers (including Richard Wright, Ralph Ellison, and James Baldwin)

primarily in literary terms, but attention is also given to the
writers' political and social ideas. The chapter on Malcolm X
describes Malcolm's transition from separatism to socialism.
By the end of his life, Malcolm believed that self-help, rather
than separatism, was more likely to effect equality. The poems
and plays of Imamu Baraka are discussed in another chapter.
Baraka's literary work is seen as "hysterical self-destruction."

Morrison, Toni. "What the Black Woman Thinks About Women's Lib."
New York Times Magazine, 22 August 1971, pp. 14-15+.

Black women have not participated in the feminist movement because they have always had the rights which white women are
seeking—to be self-supporting and to be treated as responsible
human beings. Involvement in what is essentially a "family quar-
rel" between white women and white men would lead to further
alienation of the races. Morrison suggests, however, that the
movement is shifting its emphasis from sexual rights to human
rights and that this trend has more meaning for black women.

Neal, Larry. "The Ethos of the Blues." Black Scholar 3 (Summer
1972): 42-48.

The blues are the musical manifestation of black culture. Their
appeal is universal although they first express the black experience. The blues are a folk expression that represents the collective sensibility of a people at particular stages of social, political,
and cultural development.

O'Neil, Wayne. "Politics of Bidialectalism." College English 33
(January 1972): 433-38.

By spending an inordinate amount of time on the fruitless and un-
important task of changing dialect, the educational system fails to
educate lower-class children. Thus, under the guise of offering
a chance for social betterment, education works to maintain the
status quo. Bidialectalism should be rejected because it does nothing (nor is it intended) to root out the injustices of the American
political, economic, and social system.

Porter, James A. Modern Negro Art. New York: Dryden, 1943.
Reprint. New York: Arno, 1969.

A monograph on the work of black artists since the pre-Civil War
period, emphasizing that black American artists are essentially

American, not African. However, since 1900 critics have brought
pressure on black artists to produce primitive art as their "natural" style. The period from 1930 to 1943 was less exclusively racial in character than the Harlem Renaissance, although folk culture
was still a prime source of inspiration.

Poussaint, Alvin F. "The Negro American: His Self-Image and Integration." Journal of the National Medical Association 58 (November 1966): 419-23.

Blacks suffer from many problems of identity and negative self-
image because of racism, segregation, and discrimination. The
civil rights movement generated some positive changes, but integration does not seem to offer a solution to problems of negative
self-concept. Token integration into mainstream society may even
lead to greater identity crises for blacks. The black consciousness movement could contribute a great deal to blacks' political
and social action, and the development of black consciousness
through all-black programs could serve as an alternative to integration.

Raspberry, William. "Should Ghettoese Be Accepted?" Today's
Education 59 (April 1970): 30-31.

Ghettoese is not inferior to Standard English; it is simply "less
negotiable." Bilingualism enables a black person to negotiate in
both the black and white worlds. Some linguists recommend "total immersion" in Standard English as the means of teaching it,
while others favor a gradual transition from the nonstandard to
the standard dialect.

Redding, J. Saunders. "The Black Arts Movement in Negro Poetry."
American Scholar 42 (Spring 1973): 330-36.

Poets, as part of the movement, have not succeeded in creating
individually distinctive black thoughts and poetic modes, nor have
they successfully reclaimed the "lost" African heritage from which
they purport to draw sustenance.

Redding, J. Saunders. "The Black Revolution in American Studies."
American Studies: International Newsletter 9 (October 1970):
3-9. *

Redmond, Eugene. "Black American Epic: Its Roots, Its Writers."
Black Scholar 2 (January 1971): 15-22.

Describes the black musical, literary, and art forms that comprise the black epic.

"The Revolt of Poor Black Women. " In Lessons from the Damned: Class Struggle in the Black Community, pp. 88-111. Washington, N.J.: Times Change Press, 1973.

In this essay on the development of political consciousness among black women, the authors state that many black women did not adopt the black power and unity ideology because they realized that there is a strong class system within black society. They write that "the dream of black nationhood has often been used, in Africa, to exploit poor Africans and African women. " As long as nationhood is based on capitalism, it will not help women attain their rights.

Safa, Helen Icken. "The Case for Negro Separatism. " Urban Affairs Quarterly 4 (September 1968): 45-63.

Slavery stripped the black of his African cultural heritage, and racial barriers have prevented him from assimilating into American society. There is a lack of community solidarity in the ghetto (the author analyzes why this is so); and therefore separatism, which attempts to organize the black community on the basis of sense of racial pride and identity, is a necessary prelude to integration.

Shockley, Ann Allen. "The Negro Woman in Retrospect: A Blueprint for the Future. " Negro History Bulletin 29 (December 1965): 55-56+.

Black women have been degraded more completely than black men by white society, but history has also provided the necessity for black women to be capable of both raising and supporting a family. Employment, although usually at a menial level, has been more easily available to black women than to black men.

Skolnick, Jerome H. "Black Separatism. " Chicago Today 5 (Summer 1968): 17-21.

Black separatism is "black dignity" and a response to "de facto white separatism. " Blacks are forced to develop racial consciousness and to disrupt social stability in their quest for power. Although Skolnick is appalled when disruption becomes violence, he asserts that we must recognize that the needs of black people are different from those of the comfortably situated white liberal.

Smith, Holly. "Standard or Nonstandard: Is There an Answer?" Elementary English 50 (February 1973): 225-34.

Presents the arguments which claim that black English is either inferior, or different but equal; and arguments which claim that it should or should not be taught at all, or only in conjunction with Standard English.

Smitherman, Geneva. "Grammar and Goodness." English Journal 62 (May 1973): 774-78.

English dialects are mutually intelligible; therefore, bidialectalism is a futile and perhaps even racist approach to language which forces blacks to conform to white, middle-class norms thereby denying their unique expressive style. Teachers should develop the reading and communicative skills of black children.

Smitherman, Geneva. "White English in Blackface Or, Who Do I Be?" Black Scholar 4 (May-June 1973): 32-39.

The differences between black English and Standard English are cultural, not structural. The heart of the language controversy is the underlying political nature of the school system, which requires black students to adopt the vocabulary, and therefore the values, of white society.

The Speeches of Malcolm X at Harvard. Edited, with an introductory essay, by Archie Epps. New York: William Morrow, 1969.

These speeches of Malcolm X were delivered at Harvard University on three occasions: on March 24, 1961, during his period of deep involvement with the Black Muslims; on March 18, 1964, shortly after his resignation from the Muslims; and on December 16, 1964, after his return from Africa. Thus, the speeches reflect the evolution of his position on separatism. Although he remained a revolutionary, his position in December, 1964, was less dogmatically sectarian and more secular than it had been previously.

Strickland, Dorothy S. "Black Is Beautiful vs. White Is Right." Elementary English 49 (February 1972): 220-23.

Adherents of the "white is right" philosophy characterize the speech of disadvantaged blacks as linguistically deficient; the "black is beautiful" people advocate acceptance of the nonstandard dialect and its use as a base for school instruction. Although no dialect is intrinsically better than any other, the "prestige" dialect of a given culture is necessary for educational, economic, and social success in that culture and therefore should be required.

Thorne, Richard. "Integration or Black Nationalism: Which Route Will Negroes Choose?" Negro Digest 12 (August 1963): 36-47.

Thorne opts for black nationalism on cultural grounds: predominant social values should reflect Pan-Africanist values, but this is not likely to happen in an integrated society.

Toliver-Weddington, Gloria. "The Scope of Black English." Journal of Black Studies 4 (December 1973): 107-114.

Black English, not recognized as a consistent linguistic pattern until 1964, is still rejected by segments of the black community as well as by the dominant culture. Since linguists accept black English as a legitimate system, blacks should be encouraged to speak it exclusively.

Turner, Henry M. "God Is a Negro." Voice of Mission (February 1, 1898): 75-81.

The theme "God Is a Negro" strengthens black pride and dignity, which can best be advanced by rejecting American society and culture through emigration.

Tyler, Robert. "The Musical Culture of Afro-America." Black Scholar 3 (Summer 1973): 22-27.

Black music is accessible to all black people because of its cultural and social origins. American music created from African roots has qualities which are lacking in European-derived music. The roots of black music should be emphasized because such music will become an increasingly important component of Afro-American culture.

Walters, Hubert. "Black Music and the Black University." Black Scholar 3 (Summer 1972): 14-21.

Black music should be an aspect of the struggle for black liberation, but music educators do not have a positive viewpoint concerning the black heritage. Black universities have been especially remiss in giving black music the attention it deserves.

Ward, Francis, and Ward, Val Gray. "Black Artist—His Role in the Struggle." Black Scholar 2 (January 1971): 23-32.

When social struggle is on the rise, so are black literature and art. The black artist should work to advance the struggle for liberation through the creation of art and through criticism, propaganda, activism, and fund-raising.

Williams, Maxine. "Why Women's Liberation Is Important to Black Women." In Black Women's Liberation, by Maxine Williams and Pamela Newman, pp. 3-11. New York: Pathfinder Press, 1970.

Black and other Third World women need to build alliances among themselves to speak and work against the oppression of black women as blacks, as workers, and as women.

Wright, Nathan. Black Power and Urban Unrest: Creative Possibilities. New York: Hawthorn, 1967. *

Wright, Richard. White Man, Listen! Garden City, N. Y. : Doubleday, 1957.

Lectures on the emotional relationships among Africans, American blacks, and whites, in psychological rather than social terms. Writing a few years after the Brown decision and at the beginning of the contemporary civil rights movement, Wright asserts in "The Literature of the Negro in the United States" that as the position of blacks in America improves, their literature becomes less concerned with themes of identity and race.

4. EDUCATION: SEGREGATION AND DESEGREGATION

Elementary and Secondary Schools

Alsop, Joseph. "No More Nonsense About Ghetto Education." New Republic 157 (July 22, 1967): 13-23.

Disagrees with the viewpoint of the Civil Rights Commission report, Racial Isolation in the Public Schools, and Judge James Skelley Wright's decision concerning the District of Columbia's schools. Advocates making the ghetto schools productive first and then preparing for desegregation only when it can be accomplished successfully. (See rejoinder from Robert Schwartz et al. and Brown decision.)

Barbaro, Fred. "The Newark Teachers' Strike." Urban Review 5 (January 1972): 3-10.

The community control concept must be reexamined in its application to cities in which blacks are the majority. The question that emerges from the Newark teachers' strike is: what is to prevent whites as the new minority from seizing the community control concept to advance white goals and frustrate black attempts to consolidate power?

Barbour, Floyd B., ed. The Black Seventies. Boston: Porter Sargent, 1970. *

Bell, Derrick. "NAACP: Faith and an Opportunity." Freedomways 13 (Fourth Quarter 1973): 330-34.

The education of inner-city black children, not the theory of integration, should be the main objective of the NAACP. Bell approves of the direction taken by the Atlanta branch of the NAACP in its acceptance of a minimal school integration plan combined with an extensive hiring program for black supervisors and administrators. The suspension of the Atlanta branch is an indication of the blind and futile idealism characteristic of the national NAACP's dealings with racist American society.

Billings, Charles E. "Black Activists and the Schools." High School
Journal 54 (November 1970): 96-107.*

"Black English: Route or Roadblock to Racial Progress?" Race Relations and Industry 9 (February 1974): 1-4.*

"Black Studies and Black Separatism." In Racism and American Education: A Dialogue and Agenda for Action, edited by Harold Howe,
pp. 62-82. New York: Harper and Row, 1970.*

Bolner, James, and Vedlitz, Arnold. "The Affinity of Negro Pupils for
Segregated Schools: Obstacle to Desegregation." Journal of Negro
Education 40 (Fall 1971): 313-21.

A study of black secondary school pupils in Louisiana who remained in a segregated school despite a freedom of choice plan indicates that school and racial affinity were the primary reasons for
voluntary segregation. The authors doubt the success of school
desegregation effected through pairing, bussing, or zoning if consideration is not given to the factor of school attachment as a psychological need.

Briggs, Albert A. "Educational Decision-Making." National Association of Secondary School Principals Bulletin 53 (May 1968): 176-80.

Local, not national, control has always been a feature of public education; the black demand for community control is justified because it fits into the mainstream pattern.

Brown et al. v. Board of Education of Topeka et al. 347 U.S. 483
(1954). In Argument: The Oral Argument Before the Supreme
Court in Brown v. Board of Education of Topeka, 1952-55,
edited by Leon Friedman, pp. 325-31. New York: Chelsea House,
1969.

The final decision on merits overturns the 1896 Supreme Court decision, Plessy v. Ferguson, which allowed racially separate facilities to be maintained as long as they were "substantially equal."
This seminal decision declares that educational facilities, segregated on the basis of race, are "inherently unequal" and therefore
in violation of the Fourteenth Amendment.

Browne, Robert S. "The Challenge of Black Student Organizations."
Freedomways 8 (Fall 1968): 325-33.

Discusses the sudden and drastic reversal of the manner in which
black students view themselves and the reasons for the wave of
black student confrontations. There is a new temper sweeping black
Americans generally, and this group self-awareness is creating a

restructuring of blacks' self-image. Black students are at the center of this new mood.

Caliguri, Joseph P. "Black Power and Black Students in Kansas City." Integrated Education 10 (January-February 1972): 41-48.

This article describes a study which sought to determine the attitudes of secondary school students to the concept of black power. Results showed that most students had positive feelings about the concept, but were unable to give it more than a general and amorphous meaning.

"CBE Interviews: Kenneth B. Clark." Council for Basic Education Bulletin 14 (November 1969): 8-18. *

Clark, Kenneth B. "The Dangerous Inefficiency of Racially Separated Schools." In Integration and Separatism in Education, edited by Samuel Goldman and Peter L. Clark, pp. 9-18. Syracuse: Syracuse University Press, 1970.

A description of the author's goals for the education of black children. They should be educated in an interracial milieu, which reinforces their sense of worth and well-being. "All the available evidence," he asserts, "supports the contention that children will be rejected if you attempt to educate them in a setting that concretizes their feelings of rejection."

Clark, Kenneth B. "Public School Segregation in the Seventies." New South 27 (Summer 1972): 21-28.

An examination of the present forms of resistance to public school desegregation, among them the growth of black separatism. This review and examination are necessary in order to plan strategies for effective desegregation of public schools during the seventies.

Cobbs, Price. "The Black Revolution and Education." National Association of Secondary School Principals Bulletin 53 (May 1969): 3-18.

Black people have always had the feeling that education would make them full Americans. Blacks now realize the extent of the duplicity of the educational system which has promised so much and delivered so little. They are now demanding that if there is to be a change in the status of blacks in American society, it must be done through a change in the national character. It is the responsibility of educators to renounce the racist traditions of American education and make education humane for all Americans.

62 / INSTITUTIONAL AND PSYCHOLOGICAL DIMENSIONS

Daniels, Deborah K. , ed.   Education by, for and about African Americans: A Profile of Several Black Community Schools. Lincoln:
University of Nebraska, Nebraska Curriculum Development Center, 1972.

> Describes one all-black school at each educational level that has
> succeeded in educating black children. Information on the back-
> ground, methods, and goals of these schools is included. The
> schools hold in common the idea that the public schools must be
> replaced or supplemented with all-black independent schools.

Day, Noel A. "The Case for All-Black Schools." Harvard Educational
Review 38 (Winter 1968): 134-41.

> Although studies have shown that Negro children perform better in
> racially and socially integrated settings, disparities in the
> achievement levels of Negro and white children still exist. The
> author suggests that these disparities may be caused by movement,
> that is taking Negro children out of their familiar milieu, the
> black community. This movement seems to say something nega-
> tive to children about the worth of themselves, their families, and
> their community. Such remedies as compensatory education pro-
> grams, community control, and league-of-metropolitan schools
> would not be as effective as all-black schools.

Douglass, Frederick. "Letter to W. J. Wilson, August 8, 1865." In
The Life and Writings of Frederick Douglass, edited by Philip S.
Foner, 4 vols. Vol. 4, pp. 171-74. New York: International Pub-
lishers, 1955.*

DuBois, W. E. B. "Does the Negro Need Separate Schools?" Journal
of Negro Education 4 (July 1935): 328-35. Reprinted in W. E. B.
DuBois: A Reader, edited by Meyer Weinberg, pp. 278-88. New
York: Harper and Row, 1970.

> DuBois concludes that, other things being equal, mixed schools
> provide a more natural basis for education than separate schools.
> But within a segregated society, the alternative to segregated
> schools is no education at all for blacks. Since he does not see
> integrated schools as a likelihood in the near future, DuBois en-
> courages blacks to improve the quality of education provided in
> separate schools.

Frelow, Robert D. "The Berkeley Plan for Desegregation." Unpublished paper, 1969.

> While separatism is "physically and psychologically untenable to
> most Americans, integration as it has been traditionally defined
> (i. e. , some notion of racial proximity out of which blacks through

processes of osmosis acquire the dominant value-systems and institutional behaviorisms acceptable to whites) is equally indefen-
sible." Frelow describes the Berkeley integration plan, which
presumes that both blacks and whites benefit from school desegregation. Results of the Berkeley plan indicate that desegregation of
school enrollments and diversification of teaching and administrative staff have resulted in greater academic achievement.

Galamison, Milton A. "Colloquy." Unpublished paper, 1968.

The schooling of black children in New York City is not education
but a malicious criminal act perpetrated by the Board of Examin-
ers, the Board of Education, and the United Federation of Teachers. Power must be taken from these institutions and given to the
communities to enable parents to interact with school personnel
and to make the schools accountable for the education of their children.

Galamison, Milton A. "Ocean Hill-Brownsville Dispute: Urban School
Crisis in Microcosm." Christianity and Crisis 28 (October 14,
1968): 239-41.

The controversy in Ocean Hill-Brownsville over the reassignment
of seventeen teachers is discussed in terms of the community as a
colony and the United Federation of Teachers and the Board of
Education as agents of the colonizer. Galamison thinks that the
only way to educate children of the community is to abolish the
colonial relationship and set up an autonomous school board with
the power to reassign incompetent or racist teachers.

Galamison, Milton A. Untitled paper, 1968.

A brief history of the failure of the integration and the rise of the
black power movement. Galamison feels that if the schools cannot
be integrated, they should be decentralized at every level. Non-
resident white teachers should not reap the profits of working in
the black community at the expense of the education of black children.

Giles, Raymond H., Jr. Black Studies Programs in Public Schools.
New York: Praeger, 1974.

Black studies appear to be a permanent part of elementary and
secondary curricula, although most programs will probably be in-
corporated into regular classes after older students have received
remediation. Curricula designed as liberation tools frequently fail,
Giles thinks, because the public schools will not allow them to be
realized. Sample curricula and case studies are included.

Gittell, Marilyn. "Decentralization Revisited." Urban Advocate 1 (Winter 1973): 20-30.

The failure of decentralization to reform the school systems of Philadelphia, Washington, D.C., Detroit, and New York City signals the need for alternate community school systems or alternate community schools.

Goldman, Samuel, and Clark, Peter L., eds. Integration and Separatism in Education. Syracuse: Syracuse University Press, 1970.

This volume includes papers from the All-University Summer Conference held at Syracuse University in 1969. Kenneth B. Clark's and John Doar's papers argue that separatism does not meet the needs of black children. Preston Wilcox, Ronald Walters, and Nathan Hare present various justifications for separatism in their papers. Paul Parks and William Birenbaum defend community control and self-determination but not separatism per se. The Clark and Wilcox papers are analyzed in this section.

Grant, William R. "Community Control vs. School Integration—the Case of Detroit." Public Interest 24 (Summer 1971): 62-79.

A history and analysis of the movement for decentralization of Detroit's public schools in 1969-70. The basic issue in the campaign was whether community control was compatible with racial integration. The answer in Detroit was no.

Grimke, Francis J. "Colored Men as Professors in Colored Institutions." A.M.E. Church Review 4 (July 1885): 142-49.*

Hamilton, Charles V. "Race and Education: A Search for Legitimacy." Harvard Educational Review 38 (Fall 1968): 669-84.

Some black parents, teachers, and students are questioning the legitimacy of educational institutions. Since attempts to improve the schools have failed, Hamilton supports those who call for community control of schools combined with close alliance between teacher and parent, as well as those who urge that the curriculum be focused more on Afro-American culture and awareness and less on basic skills.

Harlem Board of Education Organizing Committee. Proposal for an Independent Harlem School System. New York: CORE, 1967.

The New York City Board of Education has failed at teaching the children of Harlem. This committee doubts that the existing school system can be made responsible, and proposes that an independent system be set up to be accountable to the Harlem community.

Harrison, H. "Extremists and the Schools: A Context for Understanding." Educational Leadership 26 (January 1969): 335-37.

The demands of blacks for change in the educational system deserve a hearing; they are not extremist. Curriculum must be changed so that it is contemporary and relevant to the ghetto; for example, The Autobiography of Malcolm X could be substituted for Silas Marner as a tool for refining reading skills.

Haskins, Kenneth W. "A Black Perspective on Community Control." Inequality in Education 15 (November 1973): 23-34.

The community control in education movement is addressing itself not to minor reforms but to fundamental changes in schools. The movement is an outgrowth of the history of education for blacks in which integrated schools were largely unattainable. Schools must be fully autonomous from central control, financial or professional. Decentralization of schools is an inadequate solution because it is merely an administrative reform which leaves most control in the same hands. Haskins describes the program and organization of one independent, community-controlled school in Washington, D.C.

Henderson, George. "Black Nationalism and the Schools." National Elementary Principal 47 (September 1967): 14-20.

Negative attitudes of black nationalists toward public schools can be counteracted. Techniques for school-community relationships are discussed, as well as a means of counteracting negative student attitudes.

"Interview with John Hope Franklin." Urban Review 5 (September 1971): 32-37.

Franklin's views on such topics as assimilation versus separatism in the Negro community, black studies programs, the future of the Negro college, and innovations in teaching history and social studies. On black separatism he points out that this is not a new trend—it has been with us for 150 years—but the effort to strengthen the social, cultural, economic, and political aspects of the black community is more prominant today than in previous separatism movements. On black studies programs he says that there are two thrusts. One is an educational thrust in which an interdisciplinary body of knowledge is being developed to enhance understanding of the black segment of the American community. The other is an ideological, social, and political thrust which is a means of imbuing a person with a sense of pride, respect, and identity.

Jencks, Christopher. "Private Schools for Black Children." New York Times Magazine, 3 November 1968, pp. 30-31+.

Differences in educational attainment are caused by class and cultural differences, rather than by differences within schools. Consequently, the urban school crisis is primarily a political problem rather than a pedagogic one. Since militant blacks believe there is a conspiracy to keep their children stupid, the only solution is to assist black parents to set up their own schools. These separate schools would replicate the results of the public school system, thus proving to black parents that the fault is in the children rather than in the schools.

Kraft, Ivor. "Retreat to Separate but Equal." Nation 205 (November 27, 1967): 552-55.

An argument against the separate but compensatorily equal education scheme advocated by black separatists and their white supporters.

Levine, Daniel U. "Black Power: Implications for the Urban Educator." Education and Urban Society 1 (February 1969): 139-59.

Educators should support certain demands of black power groups such as making the study of black history and culture an integral part of the curriculum, giving representative citizens' groups a significant voice in educational decisions affecting their children, and devising ways for the schools to be involved in community services. The black power movement is divided, and there are aspects of the movement, such as the rhetoric and the practice of violence and separatism, that are questionable. School officials, however, should seek the positive educational gains to be derived from the movement and not ignore it completely.

Link, William R. "More Blacks, but Less Integration: Black Youth, Black Nationalism and White Independent Schools." Independent School Bulletin 29 (October 1969): 14-15.

Spontaneous racial grouping should not be discouraged, since ghetto youngsters have more in common with each other than with white children.

Longino, Charles F., and Wagoner, Jennings L. "Educational Criticism and the Transformation of Black Consciousness." Educational Forum 36 (May 1972): 499-506.*

Maynard, Robert C. "Black Nationalism and Community Schools. " In Community Control of Schools, edited by Henry M. Levin, pp. 100-14. Washington, D.C.: The Brookings Institution, 1970.

Black nationalists are using community control of schools as a means of achieving their goals of black pride, black self-determination, and alteration of the present power relationships of black to white. One of the major aspects of the black nationalist movement, in its community control phase, is the "autodidacticism of necessity, " the need for blacks to teach themselves because because whites have failed to do so.

"NAACP Suspends Atlanta Unit; Repudiates School Agreement." Crisis 80 (May 1973): 168.

A brief description of why and how the officers of the Atlanta NAACP branch were suspended becasue of a compromise plan for school integration. The plan settled for less integration but more black school administrators. The NAACP reaffirms here its commitment to fight for integration.

Pfautz, Harold W. "The Black Community, the Community School, and the Specialization Process: Some Caveats. " In Community Control of Schools, edited by Henry M. Levin, pp. 13-39. Washington, D.C.: The Brookings Institution, 1970.

One of the by-products of the civil rights movement has been group solidarity. Consequently, more ghetto residents now prefer separate black schools for their children. The author expects the inherent divisiveness of the ghetto to reassert itself.

Robinson, Isaiah E., Jr. "Preparation for Life: The Black Classroom." In Black Manifesto for Education, edited by Jim Haskins, pp. 3-15. New York: William Morrow, 1973.

Only white Americans have benefited from integration; blacks are still excluded from schools and jobs. Two separate school systems still exist in cities. The teacher's role is to develop a sense of self-worth in all students. Only black teachers have the gift to restore respect to black students. The antisocial behavior of black children can largely be ascribed to the need for defense against the segregated school environment.

Rosenthal, Robert, and Jacobson, Lenore. Pygmalion in the Classroom. New York: Holt, Rinehart and Winston, 1968.

Presents anecdotal and statistical evidence from medicine and the behavioral sciences to prove the hypothesis that children learn in direct relationship to teachers' assumptions about what they can and will do.

Russell, Carlos. "Rev. Milton A. Galamison: Man of Action." Liber-ator 3 (May 1963): 15.

An interview in which Galamison explains his belief in total inte-gration and his plan for open enrollment in New York City schools.

Russell, Michele. "Erased, Debased, and Encased: The Dynamics of African Educational Colonization in America." College English 31 (April 1970): 671-81.

The most relevant education for blacks is one which teaches them to throw off their colonial status, to defend themselves and to serve the black community.

Satterwhite, Frank J., ed. Planning an Independent Black Educational Institution. New York: Afram Associates, 1971.

Report of a conference in Oakland, California, at which represent-atives discussed the need for independent black educational institu-tions. Nearly all black children attend school in white-controlled institutions where they are taught European nationalism rather than the skills they need to build a Pan-African culture. Thus, inde-pendent black institutions should be established which would be ac-countable to the black community and would provide black children with identity, purpose, and direction.

Schwartz, Robert, et al. "Fake Panaceas for Ghetto Education." New Republic 157 (September 23, 1967): 16-19; and 157 (January 6, 1968): 15-18.

A reply to Joseph Alsop's article, "No More Nonsense About Ghet-to Education." Emphasizes that interracial contact is an essential ingredient for quality education and the full racial desegregation of American public schools must be the goal.

Sizemore, Barbara A. "Is There a Case for Separate Schools?" Phi Delta Kappan 53 (January 1972): 281-84.

According to Sol Tax's inclusion/exclusion model, integration would create jobs for those in power and is thus inimical to black interests. In order to achieve inclusion, blacks must use a sep-aratist model called power-inclusion model. Sizemore points out that this is especially relevant in education where integration and community control have been ineffective.

Slater, Jack. "Learning Is an All-Black Thing." Ebony 26 (September 1971): 88-92.

Description of the all-black Nairobi Day Schools and Nairobi College in East Palo Alto, California.

Smith, Holly. "Standard or Nonstandard: Is There an Answer?" Elementary English 50 (February 1973): 225-34. *

Smith, Paul M. "Black Activists for Liberation, Not Guidance." Personnel and Guidance Journal 49 (May 1971): 721-26.

Describes the role of a black activist who must function as a role model for black children. Smith believes that activists must take over functions which are performed inadequately by the white power structure, particularly in education.

Smitherman, Geneva. "White English in Blackface or, Who Do I Be?" Black Scholar 4 (May-June 1973): 32-39. *

Stember, Charles Herbert. "Evaluating Effects of the Integrated Classroom." Urban Review 2 (June 1968): 3-4, 30-31.

An argument for sanctioning self-segregation by minority groups. The reasons are: the minority must have the right to decide for itself what is best for it and must be allowed to pursue its own methods to achieve its goals. In addition, voluntary segregation in schools and housing may be warranted because integration has been so slow in coming.

Stimpson, Catherine R. "Black Culture/White Teacher." Change in Higher Education 2 (May-June 1970): 35-40.

White people misread black literature by judging it on the basis of warped criteria. Therefore, the only people qualified to teach black literature are blacks.

U. S. Commission on Civil Rights. Racial Isolation in the Public Schools. 2 vols. Washington, D.C.: U.S. Government Printing Office, 1967.

Illustrates the degree of racial isolation in public schools (approaching 90 percent in metropolitan areas) documented by the 1960 census. As a result of this segregation, the outcomes of education for black and white Americans are markedly different; educational disparities result in lower earnings and lower occupational levels over a lifetime. Desegregation is a more effective remedy than compensatory education, which can be directed toward segregated groups.

Wicker, Tom. "The Danger of White Liberalism." New York Times, 15 February 1968, p. 42.

Black power challenges the doctrine of white liberalism. Convinced that whites will only support a second-class integration, young blacks want to manage their own communities and desire "separate but equal" schools.

Wilcox, Preston R. "Black Control: In Search of Humanism." In Integration and Separatism in Education, edited by Samuel Goldman and Peter L. Clark, pp. 19-31. Syracuse: Syracuse University Press, 1970.

The issue of integration or separatism in education is less important than the right to control the content and form of the educational experience. The move for black control of schools is not racist, but an attempt to remove racists from control so that education for humanism can take place.

Wilcox, Preston R. "The Community-Centered School." In The Schoolhouse in the City, edited by Alvin Toffler, pp. 97-109. New York: Praeger, 1968.

The drive by the black community for the control of their schools is concerned less with social integration than with effective education. To achieve this goal, the school must not only be controlled by the black community but must also function as an acculturation tool, an educational instrument, and a community center.

Wilcox, Preston R. "Education for Black Liberation." New Generation 5 (Winter 1969): 17-21.

The purpose of education is to teach children skills to shape the conditions of their work, not to fit into a dehumanized work force. The community control movement, because it is neither racist nor separatist, has the philosophy and the means to achieve this end.

Wilkinson, Doreen H. Community Schools: Education for Change. Boston: National Association of Independent Schools, 1973.

Black independent schools are a necessary alternative to the inadequate public school system. Wilkinson describes several such schools set up in the late sixties. Many of these schools are run competently without interference from middle-class professionals from the suburbs, and are able to teach basic skills as well as pride in the black heritage.

Young, Whitney M., Jr. "Minorities and Community Control of the
   Schools." Journal of Negro Education 38 (Summer 1969): 285-90.

   Blacks who demand local control for their schools are asking no
   more than residents of white suburbs. Young proposes safeguards
   to deal with the danger of separatist takeover, such as community
   councils elected or appointed by local and federal governments.
   He also points out that community control may perpetuate segregation.

Higher Education

Abram, Morris. "The Eleven Days at Brandeis—As Seen From the
   President's Chair." New York Times Magazine, 16 February
   1969, pp. 28, 29+.

   Describes the takeover of Brandeis's main building by black students. To end the strike, President Abram agreed to a number of
   nonnegotiable demands, including the establishment of an on-
   campus center for black students, the enlargement of the black
   studies program into a full department, and the recruitment of
   more black students and black faculty.

Anthony, Earl. The Time of the Furnaces. New York: Dial, 1971.

   A case study of the black student movement at San Fernando Valley State College, and the issues involved in creating an Afro-
   American studies department and a black student union.

Ballard, Allen B. The Education of Black Folk: The Afro-American
   Struggle for Knowledge in White America. New York: Harper and
   Row, 1973.

   A discussion of the paradoxes and contradictions in the black struggle for education; the persistent efforts of black educators to develop strategies for higher education in a segregated society; and
   the conflict which took place when institutions admitted large numbers of black youth. Ballard asserts the need for black people to
   be cognizant of the unresolved ideological dilemma within the black
   community: whether to fight for integration or separation, and
   warns against allowing this dilemma to deflect appropriate strategies beneficial to black people.

Beckham, Edgar F. "What We Mean by the Black University." College Board Review 71 (Spring 1969): 10-15.

   Describes the proposal for a black university, conceived by the
   National Association of Afro-American Education. The black

university would be a center for the production of new knowledge about blacks and a means for the dissemination of that knowledge. Also suggested are cooperative programs in black studies.

Bell, Daniel. "Columbia and the New Left." In Confrontation: the Student Rebellion and the Universities, edited by Daniel Bell and Irving Kristol, pp. 67-107. New York: Basic Books, 1969.

This article about the 1968 uprising at Columbia deals briefly with the role of the black coalition of students from Columbia and other schools, and with CORE and SNCC. When blacks decided to take control of the Hamilton Hall seizure, the charge of institutional racism became the central issue of the conflict, and the administration was embarrassed because the Columbia black community was separating itself from the university.

"Black Colleges: Vital Part of American Education." Engage/Social Action 2 (December 1974): 17-48.

Describes programs and attitudes at eight black colleges affiliated with the United Methodist Church and the United Church of Christ. These colleges provide higher education for many black students who otherwise would not receive it. In addition, black colleges meet the peculiar needs of their students by providing positive role models with their predominantly black faculty, as well as personal attention for poorly prepared students.

"Black Leaders Speak Out on Black Education." Today's Education 58 (October 1969): 25-32.

The editors of Today's Education invited black educators and other black leaders to comment on four questions on education for blacks, including black separatism and its reflection of black dissatisfaction with higher education. The respondents are J. Otis Cochran, Joseph C. Duncan, Nathan Hare, William L. Smith, Sidney F. Walton, Roy Wilkins, Laura Campbell, and Price Cobbs.

"Black Studies: An American View." Times Educational Supplement no. 2956 (January 14, 1972): 12.

Black studies programs contain an inherent contradiction: they are expected to provide materials for positive group identification by giving special attention to subjects long ignored, a method of inquiry which cannot sustain the "corrosive skepticism" that marks the teaching of other aspects of social or political history. The author sees separatism as a response to this contradiction. The primary result of separatism is to make the black studies program "an academic ghetto sealed off from the intellectual currents and values of the larger institution."

"Black Studies and Black Separatism. " In Racism and American Education: A Dialogue and Agenda for Action, edited by Harold Howe,
pp. 62-82. New York: Harper and Row, 1970.

The President's Commission for the Observance of Human Rights
Year, 1968, held a conference on Martha's Vineyard in July, 1968,
to explore the role of education in combating racial prejudice. Participants, including Jerome Wiesner, Eli Ginsberg, Harold Howe,
C. Vann Woodward, Erik Erikson, Kenneth B. Clark, Lisle Carter,
Christopher Edley, Kenneth Boulding, Franklin Roosevelt, Clyde
Ferguson, Donald Ogilvie, and Thomas Pettigrew, discussed in
part the ideological, psychological, educational, and social implications of black studies and black separatism.

"The Black University: A Revolutionary Educational Concept Designed
to Serve the Total Black Community. " Negro Digest 17 (March
1968): 4-96.

All of the contributors to this special issue (Gerald McWorter,
Darwin T. Turner, Stephen E. Henderson, J. Herman Blake,
Vincent Harding, and Nathan Hare) criticize the way in which
blacks have been educated in black colleges and in predominantly
white colleges. This mis-education has resulted in a lack of self-
confidence on the part of blacks and an attitude of contempt for the
black community.

Blassingame, John W. "Black Studies: An Intellectual Crisis. " American Scholar 38 (Autumn 1969): 548-61.

Black studies programs can function well if they are rationally organized and as intellectually respectable as other college programs. The early programs Blassingame evaluates were plagued
by confused objectives. Even when qualified instructors, white or
black, could be found, they were required to teach and counsel so
many students that their research suffered. Many white schools
have deliberately organized ill-conceived programs because they
are intended solely for black students. He thinks that black students' demands for separate facilities are incomprehensible, since
black students have no reason to trust what they call the "white
power structure" to provide separate but equal facilities.

Blassingame, John W. , ed. New Perspectives on Black Studies.
Urbana, Ill. : University of Illinois Press, 1971.

A collection of essays compiled in an effort to answer some of the
complex questions posed by black studies. Some of the essays are
analyzed elsewhere in this bibliography.

Borders, William. "Racial Diversity Unsettles Wesleyan." New York Times, 31 January 1969, pp. 41, 42.

Describes the tensions at Wesleyan University after the black enrollment was increased to 9 percent of the total student body. Black students reported a great deal of subtle racism among white students. The Afro-American Society lobbied successfully for a separate center on campus, which houses a few black students and provides study space and a library. Wesleyan's president, Edwin D. Etherington, defends the university's agreement to set up the separate facility on the grounds that Wesleyan is seeking to be a microcosm of the larger society, and clashes are to be expected.

Brimmer, Andrew F. "The Black Revolution and the Economic Future of Negroes in the United States." American Scholar 38 (Autumn 1969): 629-43.

Brimmer makes a favorable prognosis for greater participation by blacks in the national economy, but he is disturbed by the increasing number of college administrators who cater to the wishes of black students for black studies courses that emphasize urban problems, eradication of racism, and Afro-American culture. Important as these areas are, they should not be substituted for a thorough grounding in basic skills and in the hard and social sciences. The future job market will be accessible to those who have acquired marketable skills and who are confident in their ability to compete.

Brooke, Edward W. "Black Higher Education and Its Challenges." Equal Opportunity 8 (Winter 1974-75): 42-51.

In this article, based on a commencement address at Virginia Union University, Brooke calls for continued private and federal support for black institutions. Despite partial integration at white institutions, black schools will educate greater numbers of black students and provide special services to enable these students to overcome previous educational deficiencies. Black schools must close the gap between the number of whites and blacks with professional training.

Bullock, Henry A. "The Black College and the New Black Awareness." Daedalus 100 (Summer 1971): 573-602.

Black colleges, established and operated under the assumption that American blacks should be trained to enter the mainstream of American life, have failed in this effort because of the persistence and pervasiveness of racism. Since the emergence of black power ideology and the civil rights movement, however, a new black awareness has challenged the rationale of the black college. It is now necessary for black colleges to use this new ethos to help students constructively deal with the barriers of racism and at the same time participate in both black and white cultures.

Caldwell, Earl. "College Chiefs Urge Ethnic Centers." New York Times, 28 June 1969, p. 15.

A closed conference of college presidents, chancellors, deans, and other educators held to discuss higher education for nonwhite students recommended the establishment of huge regional ethnic studies centers. These centers would be located in large cities and would be attended and staffed by nonwhites. They would replace individual ethnic studies centers on each campus.

Cardoso, Jack J. "Ghetto Blacks and College Policy." Liberal Education 55 (October 1969): 363-72.

Discusses the reaction of the male black student to a liberal, white, male-oriented campus. Black separatism is a natural response to a hostile situation, but it is not a justified reaction. The result of separatist postures is that any communication between blacks and the university is lost. "Colleges must accept the confrontation with the totality of black involvement, and its 'demands' must be received with the rationality that liberal minds pride themselves in exercising. Should the college prove to be as hostile as blacks believe, then irrationality becomes reason."

Clark, Kenneth B. "The Booby Trap of Black Separatism." Speech delivered at the University of Chicago, May 1972.*

Clark, Kenneth B. "A Charade of Power: Black Students at White Colleges." Antioch Review 26 (Summer 1969): 145-49.

Black students should realize that by demanding separate facilities on integrated campuses they are not achieving any control over the majority of power held by university officials. Furthermore, whites who submit to such demands are participating in another manifistation of racism.

Clark, Kenneth B. "Letter of Resignation from Board of Directors of Antioch College." In Black Studies, Myths and Realities, by Martin Kilson et al., pp. 32-34. New York: A. Philip Randolph Educational Fund, 1969.

In acceding to the demands of black students for the Afro-American Studies Institute, Antioch College is reneging on its own educational and moral mandate by permitting and financially supporting a segregated facility. Clark writes: "There is absolutely no evidence to support the contention that the inherent damage to human

beings of primitive exclusion on the basis of race is any less dam-
aging when demanded or enforced by the previous victims than
when imposed by the dominant group. There is absolutely no valid
basis by which educational institutions can or should make any distinctions on the basis of race or color."

Clark, Kenneth B. Letter to Edward to Edward H. Levi, Provost,
University of Chicago, May 14, 1968.

This letter is in response to a request for Clark's opinion on the
demand of some black students at the University of Chicago for an
all black dormitory. The demand on the part of the students for
self-imposed forms of racial separatism is as insidious as that of
involuntary segregation. The university's acquiescence to these
demands of voluntary segregation cannot be condoned on either
moral, educational or legal grounds.

Clark, Kenneth B. Letter to Robert Goheen, President, Princeton
University, January 31, 1972.

A distinction is made here between traditional racism, where
minorities were excluded from institutions, roles, and activities,
and "transitional racism," a newer form in which the minority
group is accepted but not on the same terms as the dominant group.
Transitional racism is often expressed in "do-gooding," using
"double standards of judgment," and "oversolicitousness."

Cleaver, Eldridge. "Education and Revolution." Black Scholar 1
(November 1969): 44-52.

Black separatism (as it is expressed in black studies programs) is
deplored by the ruling class because it is revolutionary. Separatism represents an exploited class's preparation to overthrow its
oppressors.

Cleveland, Bernard. "Black Studies and Higher Education." Phi
Delta Kappan 51 (September 1969): 44-46.

Describes the goals and methods of black studies programs, along
with the results of a study of universities with existing or planned
black studies programs. Administrators should accept demands
for separatism in housing and black studies departments because
the trend toward separatism is probably temporary and may be an
attempt to solve the problems of discrimination.

Coles, Flournoy. "Black Studies in the College Curriculum." Negro
Educational Review 20 (October 1969): 106-13.

Conceding to ill-conceived requests for black studies and black
curricula becomes a convenient and cheap means for the white

majority to assuage its conscience. The black students are short-changed in the long haul. Coles is in agreement with student protests against the insensitivity of most college administrators to the real needs of college students, but opposes the false and dangerous impression among students that they can effect social change by disruption.

Crowl, John A. "Black Studies: The Bitterness and Hostility Lessen, but Criticism Persists." Chronicle of Higher Education 6 (May 30, 1972): 6-7.

Describes the current status of the black studies movement in higher education. The best available estimates suggest that about two hundred institutions have some sort of black studies program, and that another four hundred offer courses in black history or culture. Most programs that have existed for three or four years have been academically oriented rather than ideological. However, some black educators feel that the programs have been poorly conceived and planned and that their quality is low. Other continuing problems are the lack of qualified faculty members (and demands that a teacher must be black to qualify) and the need to ensure that black studies programs are not the only place on campus where there are black teachers.

Cudjoe, Selwyn. "Needed: A Black Studies Consortium." Liberator 9 (September 1969): 14-16.

A call for the establishment of regional centers of Afro-American studies.

Dickinson, James C. "The Case for Black Student Power." National Association of Student Personnel Administrators 6 (April 1969): 189-200.

A description of the major problems of black students attending predominantly white colleges and universities. Several steps are suggested to achieve a productive encounter between black and white students and staff: education of the student personnel staff and white students; development of a rationale by the university administration to allow for black-only facilities; and recruitment of black staff.

Dillon, Merton L. "White Faces and Black Studies." Commonweal 91 (January 30, 1970): 476-79.

Evaluates the demand of black students for only black teachers in black studies programs. Dillon regrets the growth of separatism in the university, but cannot see a way around it.

DuBois, W. E. B. "The Negro College." Crisis 40 (August 1933): Reprinted in W. E. B. DuBois: A Reader, edited by Meyer Weinberg, pp. 177-86. New York: Harper and Row, 1970.

Only higher education can train American blacks to protect themselves and fight racial prejudice. All-black colleges are necessary because blacks are almost universally excluded from white colleges and universities.

Dunbar, Ernest. "The Black Revolt Hits the White Campus." Look 31 (October 31, 1967): 27-31.

Describes the self-segregation movement among black students on predominantly white campuses as an influence of the black nationalist movement.

Dunbar, Ernest. "The Black Studies Thing." New York Times Magazine, 6 April 1969, pp. 25-26.

Focuses on the planning for Cornell University's black studies program. Demands for autonomous black studies and separate living facilities followed shortly after the university began to recruit larger numbers of black students. Dunbar quotes several professors at Cornell and other schools on the issues of black studies, separatism, and autonomy.

Durley, Gerald L. "A Center for Black Students on University Campuses." Journal of Higher Education 40 (June 1969): 473-76.

Proposes campus centers for black students as a therapeutic environment. One function of a center should be tutoring, but the primary purpose should be counseling to build a positive identity in students.

Edwards, Harry. "The Return to the Campus." In Black Students, pp. 64-73. New York: Free Press, 1970.

Black students' demands for separate facilities on predominantly white campuses are legitimate. Black students have never been truly integrated on white campuses and by demanding separate facilities they believe that they will surmount the racist practices and activities of American education.

Engel, Robert, and Willett, Lynn H. "Educational Implications of Black Studies." Improving College and University Teaching 19 (February 1971): 267-69.

An examination of the implications of the black studies movement from three perspectives: philosophical, curricular, and

administrative. The authors suggest an area studies approach to
black studies, encompassing history, culture, language, politics,
and economics. They are concerned that a black studies department would carry a separate but equal connotation and discourage
potential white students.

Fisher, Miles M. "National Association for Equal Opportunity in Higher Education: Crusader for the Black College." Civil Rights Digest 3 (Spring 1970): 18-21.

The organization was established by a group of college presidents
in 1969 to represent predominantly black colleges and universities
in their attempt to continue as viable forces in American society.

Fisher, Robert A. "Ghetto and Gown: The Birth of Black Studies."
Current History 57 (November 1969): 290-94+.

An answer to the separatist trend in black studies is accomodation.
Traditionalists and militants must reach an understanding on such
basic issues as curriculum and interracial participation.

Frantz, Thomas T. "Demands of Black Students: A Mixed Bag."
National Association of Student Personnel Administrators 6 (April
1969): 223-25.

Black students make three major demands: (1) enrollment of more
black students; (2) additional jobs for black faculty, administrators, and counselors; and (3) greater black control of Afro-
American programs and special dormitories. Educators should
carefully consider demands of blacks for better jobs and opportunities but should not accede to separatist demands, for this
would perpetuate separate and unequal black and white cultures.

Furniss, W. Todd. "Racial Minorities and Curriculum Change."
Educational Record 50 (Fall 1969): 360-70.

"Demand for black studies in early 1969, often coinciding with
challenges to the legitimacy of institutional authority, rested on
assumptions about the ability of colleges to solve social and personal problems." Furniss examines these assumptions and suggests several areas where initiative and accommodation may be
productive.

Gallagher, Buell C., ed. College and the Black Student: NAACP
Tract for the Times. New York: NAACP, 1971.

An overview of the role of the black student in higher education, in
both predominantly black and white schools. Gallagher discusses
segregation, separatism, black students on white campuses, curriculum, and governance.

Genovese, Eugene D. "Black Studies: Trouble Ahead." Atlantic 223 (June 1969): 37-47.

The American university cannot afford to surrender its historical heritage and content in order to right the wrongs of the whole political and social system. In spite of the demands of black militants, black studies in the university must conform to the standards and roles that the institution has set for its effectiveness. Black studies programs in an integrated university have two tasks: (1) to provide a strong setting within which black people can train an intelligentsia to lead all levels of political and social action, and (2) to help combat the racism of white students. The university cannot, however, afford to lower its academic standards to achieve these goals, and must do so within the proper context of a university in this society.

Giles, Raymond H., Jr. Black Studies Programs in Public Schools. New York: Praeger, 1974.*

Grimke, Francis J. "Colored Men as Professors in Colored Institutions." AME Church Review 4 (July 1885): 142-49.*

Guinier, Ewart. Three articles in response to Kilson. Amsterdam News, 24 November 1973, p. A-1+; 8 December 1973, p. A-1+; 15 December 1973, p. A-5+.

Three-part response to Martin Kilson's article on black students in predominantly white universities. Guinier states that the purpose of his response is to unveil the shoddiness of Kilson's scholarship and "its organic relation to [his] stance as a defender of white power." Many of Harvard's supposedly high-risk black students become fine scholars, despite Kilson's belief that these lower-class blacks are not bright enough to be admitted to an elite university. Afro-American studies is a field particularly suited to these students' needs because it serves as a vehicle to transmit concern for liberation.

Hallman, Ralph J. "White Paper on Black Studies." California Teachers Association Journal 65 (October 1969): 10-12.

Black power and black studies are the two major strategies which propel the current black revolution. Unfortunately the substance of each strategy prevents either or both from sustaining the entire movement. The black revolution, if it is to be successful, must have a scientific-technological-intellectual power base. With this, it will become not only a black revolution but a human revolution.

Hamilton, Charles V. "Question of Black Studies." Phi Delta Kappan 51 (March 1970): 362-64.

Well-planned black studies courses must be fit into the liberal arts curriculum. "They will prepare the student to engage the total society, not to withdraw from it. One is not going to know much about how to proceed with black economic development or with black educational development or with black political development without knowing a great deal about the total economic, educational, and political systems."

Harding, Vincent. "Black Students and the Impossible Revolution." Journal of Black Studies 1 (September 1970): 75-100.

An analysis of the origins and future of the black student movement on white and black campuses. Black students in white schools should continue to reject the endemic elitism of the university, and find pathways into the black community. Students in black schools should press for the development of a "total black university."

Hare, Nathan. "The Battle for Black Studies." Black Scholar 3 (May 1972): 32-47.

Black students feel that integration served to pluck many of the strongest blacks from the group, while failing to alter the lot of the group as a whole. As a consequence, black students are presently more interested in separation as a means of achieving self-determination. Hare implies that black studies programs are important because they will prepare black students to return to their community. He describes the tactics used in the black students' strike at San Francisco State in 1968.

Hare, Nathan. "The Case for Separatism: Black Perspective." Newsweek 73 (February 19, 1969): 56.

Black studies should comprise a comprehensive, integrated body of interdisciplinary courses. The Ph. D. is not an indication of an individual's competence to teach black studies. Black colleges are physically separate, but they have not successfully developed a sense of separate identity.

Hare, Nathan. "What Black Studies Mean to a Black Scholar." College and University Business 48 (May 1970): 56-60.

In an interview, Hare states that black studies teachers should be black so they can also provide role models for black students; black students should receive priority in admission into courses; the black community should control the programs; black studies programs are not meant to turn out qualified black students, but to help blacks shake off the shackles of inferiority; black studies is not based on racism, but on revolutionary nationalism.

Harper, Frederick D. "Black Student Revolt on the White Campus." Journal of College Student Personnel 10 (September 1969): 291-95.

Black students do not want to be Xerox copies of whites and to "make it" in a white world. Rather, they want to be "black, proud, and independent." Harper calls for admission of significant numbers of black students, black teachers, black counselors, and black administrators to the university community.

Harper, Frederick D. "Media for Change: Black Students in the White University." Journal of Negro Education 40 (Summer 1971): 255-65.

Out of the legislative acts and judicial decisions of the 1950s and 1960s, many black students entered what were previously all-white universities. The subsequent clashes between the black student and the white student body and administration precipitated the need for change from the often rigid racist and impersonal stance of the university. Black students, faculty, administrators, and white students should coordinate their efforts to change the climate of the university.

Harris, William H. "The Militant Separatists in the White Academy." American Scholar 41 (Summer 1972): 366-76.*

Harvard University. Faculty of Arts and Sciences. The First Three Years of the Afro-American Studies Department, 1969-1972. Cambridge, Mass.: 1972.

An evaluation of the Afro-American Studies Department at Harvard. The report calls for substantial increase in financial support to create four additional professorships, to continue the operation of the W. E. B. DuBois Institute for Afro-American Research, and to develop graduate programs in the field.

Harvard University. Faculty of Arts and Sciences. Report of the Faculty Committee on African and Afro-American Studies. Cambridge, Mass.: 1969.

Recommendations include: the creation of an interdivisional major combining Afro-American studies with existing fields; the establishment of a social and cultural center for black students; the development of a Center for Afro-American Studies, to provide intellectual leadership for scholars and the recruitment of black graduates.

Hatch, John. "Black Studies: The Real Issue." Nation 208 (June 16, 1969): 755-58.

The author asserts that black studies in the university will not help black students overcome their sense of racial inferiority. This feeling of inferiority is inculcated at an early age and, therefore, the remedy must begin long before college. The other danger in the separatist trend in black studies programs is the attempt to use this subject matter as the theoretical, political, and cultural base for a separate black community. Unless checked, this trend could lead to apartheid.

Henshel, Ann-Marie, and Henshel, Richard R. "Black Studies Programs: Promises and Pitfalls." Journal of Negro Education 38 (February 1969): 423-29.

Black studies programs may inadvertently become a major agent of voluntary and involuntary segregation on both the social and the academic levels. This plus the possibility of staff incompetence and student unpreparedness may perpetuate the relative academic impoverishment and isolation that is now the lot of the majority of black students.

Hudson, Herman. "Black Studies: Can They Be Really Relevant?" College Management 6 (August 1971): 38-39.

Black studies can be relevant because they can provide a positive psychological reinforcement of blackness, as well as the factual base and analytic techniques for future black leaders as they reinterpret the black person's role in American society.

Ivie, Stanley D. "Are Black Studies Relevant?" Education Forum 37 (January 1973): 183-88.

Black studies are irrelevant because no philosophical structure has been developed to support their goals. Although cultural nationalism may be the stimulus behind the demand for black studies, it is not an intellectually viable philosophy. Individual subjects—black history or African geography—may be justifiable, but the separatists' demands for all-black departments oppose the liberal arts philosophy.

Jackson, Maurice. "Toward a Sociology of Black Studies." Journal of Black Studies 1 (December 1970): 131-40.

This article points out some of the significant and distinctive aspects of black studies and discusses assumptions and principles that define the discipline. Further thinking and discussion is needed to solve some of the problems and difficulties in establishing black studies programs.

Jencks, Christopher, and Riesman, David. "The American Negro College." Harvard Educational Review 37 (Winter 1967): 3-60.

Reviewed in light of historical background, the authors discuss the roles of black colleges and universities. Their assessment is that major changes are unlikely within existing academic, social, and economic frameworks, and they, therefore, suggest alternative roles for some of the colleges.

Johnson, Clayton. "The Importance of Black Colleges." Educational Record 52 (Spring 1971): 165-70.

Even though social scientists claim that some black colleges are no longer viable and cannot compete qualitatively with predominantly white colleges, there are two major reasons for maintaining and strengthening the predominantly black college. Traditionally, black colleges have trained students for morally and socially responsible roles in their communities and will continue to do so. Further, there are few predominantly white colleges willing to take the risk of admitting students with inadequate educational skills, while black colleges provide them with the necessary supports and compensatory help.

Johnson, Thomas A. "Campus Racial Tensions Rise as Black Enrollment Increases." New York Times, 4 April 1972, pp. 1, 57.

On many major American college and university campuses, racial tensions, distrust, and near-total segregation in all but classroom activities characterize the relationship between black and white students.

Johnson, Thomas A. "Colleges Scored on Segregation." New York Times, 5 April 1972, p. 49.

Reacting in an interview to the New York Times survey which noted an increase in racial tensions on major college and university campuses, Dr. Kenneth B. Clark accused administrators of encouraging racial segregation by acceding to the demands of black students for separate facilities.

Jordan, June. "Black Studies: Bringing Back the Person." Evergreen Review 13 (October 1969): 39-41+.

Black students are dehumanized by the American educational system. The only way to help them is through the establishment of black studies programs controlled and attended by blacks. It is necessary to be conscious of one's blackness first and to acquire technical skills later.

Kilson, Martin. "Anatomy of the Black Studies Movement." Massachusetts Review 10 (Autumn 1969): 718-25.

An analysis of the black studies movement within its historical context and a discussion of the dynamics of the movement. The author concludes that the establishment of black studies programs at integrated universities is one of the ways in which the university can become a major force for ridding American society of its racist ways. But if the university is to succeed, it must beware of separatist proposals from black militants who discourage white student participation in black studies and who deemphasize intellectual and academically meaningful programs.

Kilson, Martin. "Black Studies Movement: A Plea for Perspective." Crisis 76 (October 1969): 327-32.

Notes work of DuBois, Frazier, and others in Afro-American studies long before the current vogue. Black studies must include thorough grounding in economics or sociology, but the most promising road to good jobs for blacks is through scientific and technical training, rather than the humanities.

Kilson, Martin. "Blacks at Harvard: Crisis and Change." Harvard Bulletin 75 (April 1973): 24-27; (June 1973): 31-32+.

This two-part article was reprinted in a condensed form in the New York Times Magazine of 2 September 1973. Black students at Harvard have separated themselves into a white-rejecting sub-group. The impact on their academic achievement and intellectual growth has been substantial. To rectify the situation, Kilson calls for the reorganization of Harvard's Afro-American studies program; the cessation of financing of separatist activity by white colleges; the restoration of a belief among Negro students in the value of academic achievement; and depoliticization of admissions practices for black students. This article inspired a response of the chairman of Harvard's Afro-American Studies Program, Ewart Guinier.

Kilson, Martin. "Negro Separatism in the Colleges." Harvard Today (Spring 1968): 30-33.

An increasing number of black students in white colleges are joining black student associations. Most of these organizations concentrate on cultural and psychological identity, but some are militantly extreme. If ghetto riots continue to flare up, they may become violent.

Kilson, Martin, et al. Black Studies, Myths and Realities. Introduction by Bayard Rustin. New York: A. Philip Randolph Educational Fund, 1969.

In the introduction, Bayard Rustin writes that the authors of this pamphlet discuss three ways in which black studies can be misused

(1) as a pretext for separatism; (2) for image-building or for the provision of easily passable courses; and (3) as a political tool. The other authors are Andrew F. Brimmer, Kenneth B. Clark, Norman Hill, Thomas Sowell, Roy Wilkins, and C. Vann Woodward.

Lerner, Abba. "Black Studies: The Universities in Moral Crisis." Humanist 29 (May-June 1969): 9-10, 23.

Demands for black studies programs have been supported by arguments that range from the compelling to the ridiculous. Faculty and administration responses have covered as wide a spectrum. Lerner suggests a number of thoughts to keep in mind to maintain rationality in the face of emotional arguments and responses.

Lythcott, Stephen. "Black Studies at Antioch." Antioch Review 29 (Summer 1969): 149-54.

Stephen Lythcott, a black student at Antioch College, answers the charges leveled at the Antioch Black Studies program by Kenneth B. Clark. The program at Antioch is concerned with social action, concrete problems, and bringing about change in the black community. This approach, though isolationist, allows the students to be free agents to effect change for blacks in urban communities.

Mackey, James. "A Rationale for Black Studies." Social Studies 61 (December 1970): 323-25.

Defends the position that black studies courses must be strictly accountable to standards of objective scholarship, in contrast to the position which holds that objective criteria might be temporarily suspended.

Margolis, Richard J. "The Two Nations at Wesleyan University." New York Times Magazine, 18 January 1970, pp. 9+.

Documents the tensions created at Wesleyan University by the recruitment of black students which began in 1965. Separatist demands were a response to continued racism of white students. Many of the confrontations were precipitated by misunderstandings. The author believes that both black and white students were living in cocoons.

Mayhew, Lewis B. "Neighboring Black and White Colleges: A Study in Waste." Educational Record 52 (Spring 1971): 159-64.

A discussion of the social, emotional, and traditional patterns which encourage the maintenance of predominantly white and predominantly black institutions of higher learning in the same vicinity. Recommends possible ways to ease institutional relationships.

Meyers, Michael. "A Retrospective View: Black Separatism at Antioch."
<u>Civil Liberties</u> 277 (April 1971): 5.

Report by a black student who opposed the black separatist movement on the Antioch campus and the administration's support of
that movement.

Meyers, Michael. "Viewpoint: The New Black Apartheid." <u>Change</u> 4
(October 1972): 8-9.

An examination of the reasons why black students segregate themselves on predominantly white campuses and why administrators
yield to their demands.

Meyers, Michael. "Voluntary Segregation: One Viewpoint." <u>Crisis</u> 81
(January 1974): 12-124.

The resurgence of black separatism is being used by whites to perpetuate segregation and by blacks as a precarious foundation for
cultural and racial identity.

Nichols, David C., and Mills, Olive, eds. <u>The Campus and the Racial
Crisis</u>. Washington, D.C.: American Council on Education, 1970.

Papers from the 1969 annual meeting of the American Council on
Education devoted to general problems involved in opening white
campuses to black students. The authors' points of view differ
within an integrationist framework.

Obatala, J.K. "Black Studies Stop the Shouting and Go to Work."
<u>Smithsonian</u> 5 (December 1974): 46-52.

During the late 1960s boom, the typical black studies student sought
emotional release and cultural identity. By 1974, black studies
students were seeking intellectual stimulation and vocational skills.
Black studies should provide white as well as black students with
insights into the black community, and promote integration, not
separatism. The survival of black studies on campus depends upon its ability to transcend the political struggle that fostered it.

Obatala, J.K. "Where Did Their Revolution Go?" <u>Nation</u> 215 (October 2,
1972): 272-74.

Background and analysis of the black student movement. Defines
the separatist aspects of the movement as "back-door integration-
ism." The key campus issues in the 1960s were reformist, not
qualitatively different from Martin Luther King's demands; they
were merely clothed in nationalist rhetoric.

Oliver, E. D. and Sojourner, W. A. "Black Power on the Campus: Implications for Admissions Officers and Registrars." College and University 44 (September 1969): 432-38.

Black students are demanding that educational institutions structure their curriculum to educate blacks for leadership in a new social order. The authors call upon college admissions officers and registrars (whom many students consider nonpartisan with respect to policies and procedures) to become sensitive to these demands. They urge them to update their procedures as one means of reform in higher education.

Pentony, DeVere E. "The Case for Black Studies." Atlantic 222 (April 1969): 81-82+.

The major focus of black studies is to help blacks discover their identity and to prepare leaders for the black community. The emphasis on black studies may lead to some antiwhite sentiments, but the overall effect will be self-awareness and integrity on the part of blacks and a realization on the part of whites of what racism really means.

Pifer, Alan. The Higher Education of Blacks in the United States. New York: Carnegie Corporation of New York, 1973.

Following a survey of the history of higher education for blacks, the author discusses the condition and destiny of traditionally black colleges and the education of black students in predominantly white institutions. As handmaidens of the majority, white universities failed to integrate their student bodies, and faculties have not yet reconciled themselves to black people's present needs. A reconciliation can be achieved if the university is willing to share a meaningful portion of power in the governance, administration, and staffing of higher education.

Proctor, Samuel. "The College and the Urban Community: Racial Insularity and National Purpose." Liberal Education 55 (March 1969): 78-85.

A central problem faced by American society is how to salvage the idea of cultural pluralism and preserve the notion of a common national destiny. Answers to this question will require the leadership of blacks and whites using intelligence, planning, and foresight to find ways to divert the energies of black separatists and militants through training and education into productive roles in an integrated society.

Redding, J. Saunders. "The Black Revolution in American Studies."
American Studies: International Newsletter 9 (October 1970): 3-9.

Redding criticizes the reasoning of black studies advocates because
their thoughts are based on the mystique of the concept of Negritude.
He traces "the black student revolution" to the neglect of the black
experience in traditional American studies programs.

Reid, Inez Smith. "Black Studies Programs: An Analysis." In _The
Black Prism: Perspectives on the Black Experience_, pp. 181-88.
Brooklyn: Faculty Press, 1969.

A discussion of four major issues regarding the development of
black studies programs on campuses in the United States: (1) the
need for black studies; (2) the nature of an Afro-American studies
major; (3) procedures for creating a program; and (4) suggestions
for introducing special cultural affairs programs on the black experience.

Rist, Ray C. "Black Staff, Black Studies, and White Universities: A
Study in Contradictions." _Journal of Higher Education_ 41 (November 1970): 618-29.

The dilemma of a black teacher in a black studies program lies in
trying to be militant enough to maintain legitimacy with black students, but not so militant as to put himself in conflict with the
university administration. A second dilemma of many black studies programs is that the programs attempt to combine the functions
of an academic department and a counseling-tutorial role. These
contradictions must be resolved if black studies programs are to
function well. It is invalid to insist that only blacks may teach in
black studies programs, but it is plausible to insist that counselors
and tutors of low-income black students be black.

Roberts, Steven V. "Black Studies Aim to Change Things." _New York
Times_, 15 May 1969, pp. 49, 93.

Brief discussion of purposes and goals of various black studies
programs, the problem of control of the programs, and the black
brain drain.

Robinson, Armstead L.; Foster, Craig C.; and Ogilvie, Donald H., eds.
Black Studies in the University. New Haven: Yale University Press,
1969.

"This volume is the edited record of the proceedings of a symposium sponsored by the Black Student Alliance at Yale in May 1968
to discuss the intellectual and political issues encountered in developing a program of black studies." The symposium asked these
questions: Is the special study of the black experience valid? Is it

educationally responsible? And, is it socially constructive for both blacks and whites? Harold Cruse, Martin Kilson, Maulana Ron Karenga, Nathan Hare, McGeorge Bundy, and Alvin Poussaint are among the contributors.

Rustin, Bayard. "The Failure of Black Separatism." Harper's 240 (January 1970): 25-32.*

Rustin, Bayard. "Separate Is Not Equal." In Down the Line: The Collected Writings of Bayard Rustin, pp. 253-54. Chicago: Quadrangle, 1971.

The author is wholeheartedly in support of black studies, but he feels that the students' demands for separate facilities and the white students, faculty, and administrators who aid these separatist demands are seriously impairing the best interests of black people.

Simpkins, Edward. "Black Studies: Here to Stay?" Black World 24 (December 1974): 26-29.

The roots of black studies are found in the Association for the Study of Negro Life and History and the American Negro Historical Society, old and respected organizations with minimum impact. Currently black studies programs are losing their highly charged political association, but they will remain controversial as long as racism is a problem. On the whole, black studies is becoming as academically respectable as other interdisciplinary programs.

Slater, Jack. "Learning Is an All-Black Thing." Ebony 26 (September 1971): 88-92.*

Sowell, Thomas. Black Education: Myths and Tragedies. New York: David McKay, 1972.

Following an account of his own efforts to cope with racism to get an education, the author attacks the policies of many predominantly white universities that condone the hurried establishment of ill-conceived black studies programs and the admittance of ill-prepared students from the ghetto. He offers practical suggestions for quality compensatory programs and encourages educators not to overlook the capable black students from the middle class.

Sowell, Thomas. "Colleges Are Skipping Over Competent Blacks to Admit 'Authentic' Ghetto Types." New York Times Magazine, 13 December 1970, pp. 36+.

A discussion of the paradoxes of liberalism and militancy among whites and blacks in the context of expanding black enrollment in predominantly white colleges and universities.

Sowell, Thomas. "The Plight of Black Students in the United States." Daedalus 173 (Spring 1974): 179-96.

Black students who attend white colleges and universities are "mismatched upward, so that good students go where outstanding students should be going and outstanding students go where only a handful of peak performers can survive." Sowell suggests that these pressures could be relieved by more accurately matching students to suitable institutions, and by adequate financial aid. Black faculty should be hired under nondiscriminatory hiring policies, using professional criteria rather than racial quotas. Black studies programs are vulnerable to criticism from separatists as well as integrationists; a separate society would have even greater need for a well-trained technical class which black studies will not provide.

Spaights, Ernest. "Black Studies Programs: Issues and Problems." Urban Review 5 (September 1971): 38-41.

Black studies programs must remain semiautonomous because traditional universities cannot be trusted with the goal of collective black development. On the other hand, white students should not be excluded from black studies courses. Academic standards in black studies courses tend to be somewhat lower than in other departments; university administrators must require black studies programs to conform to a minimum standard.

Sundiata, I. K. "Black Studies: A Cop-Out?" Liberator 9 (April 1969): 10.

Black studies as now conceived are a link between the black man and the white man's view of history. What is needed is an all-black view of American history.

Taylor, Orlando L. "New Directions for American Education: A Black Perspective." Journal of Black Studies 1 (September 1970): 101-11.

The author calls for an overhaul of higher education to meet the needs of black students through an Afro-American studies program. This program would involve more than a few courses in history and art, but would particularly address itself to such areas as student recruiting, admissions policies, counseling, financial aid, academic policy curriculum, and community education. White America will resist black educational power because no group wants to give up its comfort and influence.

Thelwell, Mike. "Black Studies: A Political Perspective." Massachusetts Review 10 (Autumn 1969): 703-12.

Thelwell criticizes members of the "black right wing" who say that
black studies will not prepare a student to be president of General
Motors. Nothing short of civil revolution will enable a black to be
president of General Motors. The selection of qualified instructors
is one of the most important aspects of black studies. There are
few academics, white or black, who are qualified to undertake the
aggressively radical transformation of their fields that is the purpose of these programs. Black studies programs on white campuses should prohibit recruitment away from southern Negro colleges.

Turner, James. "Black Studies: Challenge to Higher Education." In
The Troubled Campus; Current Issues in Higher Education, edited
by G. Kerry Smith, pp. 201-11. San Francisco: Jossey-Bass,
1970.

A description of the African Studies and Research Center at Cornell.
The author concludes: "Our goal is to fashion skills for a purpose
and to generate knowledge for the sake of serving; to develop
scholarly, technical, and professional careers tailored to conditions and requirements of the black community."

U.S. President's Commission on Campus Unrest. Report. Washington, D.C.: U.S. Government Printing Office, 1970.

A study in 1969 by the Urban Research Corporation of 232 predominantly white campuses reported that desire for more black recognition was the principal cause of campus protests. The specific
issue was a desire for more black studies courses.

Vontress, Clemont E. "Black Studies—Boon or Bane?" Journal of
Negro Education 39 (Summer 1970): 192-201.

"As an academic discipline, black studies is a lot of mumbo jum-
bo. The objectives are elusive, the content weak, the methods
questionable, the materials pitifully inadequate, and the assessment procedures totally inappropriate." Separatism in education
threatens to further divide the races and risks creating a South
African type of society.

Weidlein, Edward R. "The Traditionally White Institutions: For Most,
Still a Long Way to Go." Chronicle of Higher Education 6 (May 30,
1972): 4-5.

At almost all white colleges which enroll more than a handful of
black students, the blacks form their own associations and often

ask to live in an all-black corridor or dormitory wing. Although they rarely challenge black students who form their own associations, many administrators feel that establishing areas in dormitories solely for black students may violate civil rights laws. Recently both the Universities of Michigan and Pennsylvania turned down requests from black students for separate housing.

Whiting, Albert N. "Apartheid in American Higher Education." Educational Record 53 (Spring 1972): 128-31.

Separatism on predominantly white campuses seems to be spreading. Many colleges and universities which have acceded to the demands of black students may not have acted wisely and should oppose "officially endorsed institutionalized ethnic and racial separatism." The American higher educational community needs to examine this new trend carefully or risk the danger of a neo-South African apartheid.

Wilcox, Preston R. "A Letter to Black Educators in Higher Education." Annals of the American Academy of Political and Social Science 404 (November 1972): 101-17.

There is no such thing as blackness in higher education in America, outside of selected private black colleges. Blacks are trained to get into white institutions which exploit their own communities. Only wholly black institutions can train blacks to function as technicians in the black community. The author recounts the experiences which led him to these beliefs.

Wilcox, Preston R. "On the Black University." Negro Digest 19 (December 1969): 19-26.

Wilcox recommends the establishment of black-controlled universities for black students. In the meantime, he suggests that students undertake private, nonaccredited explorations of aspects of black studies, including writing papers and serving the community.

Wilkins, Roy. "The Case Against Separatism: 'Black Jim Crow.'" In Black Studies, Myths and Realities, by Martin Kilson, et al., pp. 38-39. New York: A. Philip Randolph Educational Fund, 1969.

Black students are right in demanding that more blacks be admitted to predominantly white colleges and universities; that more black teachers be hired; that there is a need to study Afro-American history and culture, but they are misguided in demanding segregated buildings and dormitories.

Willie, Charles V., and Levy, Joan D. "On White Campuses, Black Students Retreat into Separatism." Psychology Today 5 (March 1972): 50-52+.

The authors found that, due to undependable support from white friends, blacks tended to stick with other blacks on white college campuses. And when the black student population is small, there is paradoxically less cohesion and more tension among blacks than when it is large. The authors also discuss interracial dating, which is more restricted for black women than for men.

Wright, Stephen J. "Black Studies and Sound Scholarship." Phi Delta Kappan 51 (March 1970): 365-68.

The elements of black studies comprise a discipline in the usual academic sense that can be taught and learned by blacks and whites academically qualified to do so; black studies programs should be organized in both black and white institutions; and the black minority must become increasingly involved in all aspects of the economic, political, educational, and cultural life of the nation.

Wright, Stephen J., et al. "The American Negro College, Four Responses." Harvard Educational Review 37 (Summer 1967): 451-68.

Wright, Benjamin Mays, Hugh M. Gloster, and Albert W. Dent criticize the assumptions, methodology, and conclusions of Jencks and Riesman's article, "The American Negro College."

5. POLITICS: COALITIONS AND ALTERNATIVES

"A. L. A. Black Caucus Program Action Committee Proposal." Black Caucus Newsletter 2 (December 1973): 5-6.

A group formed in 1970 to bring pressure on the American Library Association to respond to the disparity in the development of librarianship for blacks. Also an attempt to respond positively to the suggestions of black librarians within the A. L. A. to remedy the disparity.

Axam, John A. "The Black Caucus: A Meaningful Course of Action." In What Black Librarians Are Saying, edited by E. J. Josey, pp. 208-17. Metuchen, N. J.: Scarecrow Press, 1972.

The black caucus is a pressure group within the larger professional organization of an independent entity whose purpose is to serve the needs of its black constituents and the wider black community. Caucuses of black librarians are responsible for seeing that improved library resources become available to ghetto residents.

Baraka, Imamu Amiri. "Strategies and Tactics of an Afro-American Party." Black Politician 3 (October 1972): 40-43.

Politics provides the best strategy for the transformation of black communities into power blocs.

Baraka, Imamu Amiri. "Toward the Creation of Political Institutions for All African Peoples." Black World 21 (October 1972): 54-78.

A detailed chronology of the planning sessions for the Black Political Convention in Gary, Indiana; the convention itself; and the attempt to exert influence in the 1972 Democratic National Convention. Baraka criticizes the behavior of members of the Congressional Black Caucus, of civil rights leaders and organizers, and other politicians. He is cynical about the honesty and effectiveness of all black politicians except those who work on a purely local level. Baraka suggests that American blacks should work to bring about the unification of Africa. The ultimate goal should be to win black American influence in Africa and the support of a powerful Africa behind black Americans in the U. S.

Barbour, Floyd B. , ed. The Black Seventies. Boston: Porter Sargent, 1970.

A collection of essays which attempt to go beyond protest, rhetoric, and militance to a more humanistic exploration of the real black experience as it relates to the past, the paradoxes of the present, and the possibilities of the future.

Boggs, Grace, and Boggs, James. "The City Is the Black Man's Land." Monthly Review 17 (April 1966): 35-46.

Since blacks are becoming a majority in the cities, they should take over the leadership as have other ethnic groups. White power, however, will not let the black man run the cities, so a revolution which includes force (based on the principles of the Federation for Independent Political Action) is the only solution.

Boggs, James. The American Revolution. New York: Monthly Review Press, 1963.

Changes in the social order must proceed by means of political and economic power, and not through the major labor unions (AFL-CIO) or civil rights organizations (NAACP).

Bond, Julian. "Black Elected Officials in the South." In The Black Man in American Politics; Three Views: Kenneth B. Clark, Julian Bond, Richard G. Hatcher, pp. 19-25. New York: Metropolitan Applied Research Center, 1969.

Civil War Reconstruction facilitated gains in black political power (which the author delineates) as did the Reconstruction which followed the Second World War. The former was ended by Rutherford B. Hayes; Richard Nixon and the complacency engendered by some token gains threaten the latter. Exercise of the right to vote, accompanied by sustained, united, aggressive political action, an awareness of political realities, and race-consciousness are necessary if economic gains are to be realized.

Bond, Julian. A Time to Speak, A Time to Act: The Movement in Politics. New York: Simon and Schuster, 1972.

The Georgia State Representative writes that politics will be useful in the struggle for black equality only if it is free from party alliance or the style of machine politics. Bond visualizes the construction of a political movement which combines electoral victories with manipulation of nationalist sentiment to yield ethnic diversity. An essay on the campus revolution points out that building takeovers and demands for separate facilities are symptoms of the students' demand for basic change in both the university and the society.

Brooke, Edward W. "Minority Enterprise—the Need for Bold Initiatives and Staunch Allies." Speech to the Contractors' Association of Boston, March 2, 1974.*

Brooke, Edward W. "Our Goal Is Individual Freedom." Ebony 25 (August 1970): 160-65.

African countries have realized that separation is a means to an end rather than a goal; cooperation with other nations is necessary to make the advantages of Western society applicable to the African situation.

Brooke, Edward W. Speech to the Third Annual Dinner of the Congressional Black Caucus. Washington, D. C., September 29, 1973.

Politics can be used to achieve greater economic power for blacks. Free-floating coalitions across racial lines should be formed around pragmatic issues of common interest.

Brown, H. Rap. Die Nigger Die! New York: Dial, 1969.

These autobiographical essays reflect Brown's view of his transition from a reformer (as head of SNCC) to a nationalist. As of the conclusion of the book, his position is that ending the capitalist system is the first step in black liberation.

Carmichael, Stokely, and Hamilton, Charles V. Black Power: The Politics of Liberation in America. New York: Vintage, 1967.

Describes the black power ideology, showing where it differs from integration. Separatism is not discussed, but it is implicitly evident as a possible alternative to integration after blacks have gained power.

"The Case for an Independent Black Political Party." International Socialist Review 29 (January-February 1968): 39-55.

This is the text of a resolution passed by a national convention of the Socialist Workers Party in 1967. Black people need an independent political party because the Republican and Democratic parties are controlled by their capitalist and racist oppressors. Such a party would undermine the Democratic coalition, and thus destroy the two-party system. An independent black party must use both electoral politics and mass action as well as revolutionary politics to change the policies that affect ghetto life. Leaders should not expect sudden electoral victories, but should build up mass support gradually through careful organization and activities to help blacks in their daily life.

Clark, Kenneth B. "The Negro Elected Public Official in the Changing
American Scene." Speech delivered at the National Conference of
Negro Elected Officials, Chicago, September 30, 1967.

Black power emerged as blacks realized that the fundamental problems of racism remained despite the gains of the civil rights movement. The movement's center shifted to urban racial ghettos,
where the riots in Watts and Harlem marked the beginning of the
new era. The white backlash was a cause, not a result, of the
riots. Black power is the contemporary form of Booker T. Washington's accommodation to white America's refusal to grant equality to black Americans.

Cleaver, Eldridge. "Tears for the Pigs." Humanist 28 (March-April
1968): 7-12.

Organization and education for liberation can solve the problems of
blacks. The Black Panther Party seeks the power to implement its
ten-point program in the interest of self-control for the black community.

Ferry, William H. "Blacktown and Whitetown: The Case for a New
Federalism." Saturday Review 51 (June 15, 1968): 14-17.

Even though the idea of black manhood and dignity has become a
powerful force in American life, policies leading to more governance of blacks by whites will not solve racial problems. Negro
communities should establish autonomous institutions.

Ferry, William H. "Farewell to Integration." Center Magazine 1
(March 1968): 35-40.

Integration in America is impossible because of white resistance
and because the cities will be all black in less than a generation.
The government must soon develop a political theory and practical
arrangements to provide for peaceful coexistence with an ethnically separated minority community.

Foner, Philip, ed. The Black Panthers Speak. New York: Lippincott,
1970.

This anthology includes excerpts from the Black Panther newspaper and from speeches and writings by Huey P. Newton, Bobby
Seale, Eldridge Cleaver, David Hilliard, Fred Hampton, and
others. There is a variety of points on most issues. The most
common thrust is the demand for a pluralist society in which each
racial or ethnic group has sufficient political power.

Freeman, Linton C., and Sunshine, Morris H. <u>Patterns of Residential Segregation</u>. Cambridge, Mass.: Schenkman, 1970.

A summary of American residential segregation, in a holistic, rather than historical, view. The authors develop a preliminary theory and a computer model for ethnic residential segregation patterns.

Glasgow, Douglas. "Black Power Through Community Control." <u>Social Work</u> 17 (May 1972): 59-64.

Choosing between separatism and integration is not the main issue today for black people. The decisive issues, from a black perspective, are self-determination, community control, and achievement of power.

Gould, Geoffrey. "Soul City." <u>New Republic</u> 165 (July 3, 1971): 9-11.

The federal government's reaction to funding requests for Floyd McKissick's "audacious venture" (the establishment of an all-black new town in a depressed agricultural area of North Carolina) has been positive, but whites in neighboring towns oppose Soul City on racial grounds.

Hahn, Harlan. "Black Separatists: Attitudes and Objectives in a Riot-torn Ghetto." <u>Journal of Black Studies</u> 1 (September 1970): 35-53.

This appraisal of black separatism as a social and political movement concludes that the growth of black separatism reflects a loss of faith in established sources of legal and political power. The author states that the problems posed by this movement present serious challenges to white leadership.

Hamilton, Charles V. "Blacks and the Crisis of Political Participation." <u>Public Interest</u> 34 (Winter 1974): 188-210.

The existing political structure was developed before blacks became a viable political force. In the 1960s, when blacks began to turn to the federal government for redress of grievances, they discovered the limits of the government's federalized system. Further governmental centralization is necessary to modernize the American political process. Neither calls for local control nor revenue-sharing significantly alter the need for increased centralization to protect the rights of minorities.

Hatcher, Richard G. "The Negro in American Politics." In The Black Man in American Politics; Three Views: Kenneth B. Clark, Julian Bond, Richard G. Hatcher, pp. 26-41. New York: Metropolitan Applied Research Center, 1969.

The corporate system and the institutions and values it creates are the enemy, not racists, white politicans, or the news media. Although black elected officials must work for political reform, reform must not be the final goal; black nationalism and an independent black political organization must be developed to revolutionize the working class.

Henderson, Lenneal. "Engineers of Black Liberation." Black Politician 1 (April 1970): 12-13.

An overview of the status of black political scientists, and an assessment of the origins, activities, and agenda of the Black Caucus of the American Political Science Association and the Conference of Black Political Scientists.

Hentoff, Nat. "Applying Black Power: A Speculative Essay." Evergreen Review 10 (December 1966): 44-47, 64.

Blacks need to develop a meaningful strategy and program of self-help in their segregated communities as a first step to becoming a part of "the pluralism of power."

Hunt, Deryl G. "The Viable Black Community." Black Politician 3 (October 1971): 35-39.

Concerned with finding an answer to the problem of racial strife in America, Hunt argues for greater political participation at the local level by blacks and offers community control as the means through which greater political participation may take place. He warns that blacks may turn to a separatist strategy if greater political participation is not forthcoming.

"Integrated or Separate: Which Road to Progress?" New Generation 49 (Fall 1967): 1-28.*

Jones, James M. "The Political Dimensions of Black Liberation." Black Scholar 3 (September 1971): 67-75.

The liberation which black politics will help to achieve consists, in part, of psychological liberation from the dominance of white culture.

Jones, Mack H. "A Note from a Black Political Scientist." Black
   Politician 2 (April 1971): 24-25.

   Statement presented to the American Political Science Association
   Committee on the Status of Blacks in the Profession on the occasion of Jones's resignation from the committee to help organize
   the National Conference of Black Political Scientists. Jones proposes two ways in which black people can break their dependent
   relationship with whites: by a theoretical linking of their struggle
   for liberation with that of other third world peoples; and by creating within white-dominated groups black independent social and intellectual structures free of white control.

Killens, John O. "The Artist and the Black University." Black Scholar 1 (November 1969): 61-65.

   A description of the evolution of the black artist's role in defining
   goals, principles, and strategies for the civil rights movement
   and an explanation of a "Black Communiversity," concerned with
   consciousness-raising for black unity and making black literature
   and art relevant to living and liberation.

Lasch, Christopher. "Black Power: Cultural Nationalism as Politics."
   In The Agony of the American Left, pp. 117-68. New York:
   Knopf, 1969.

   A discussion of the meaning of black power and an analysis of its
   major proponents and strategies. Black power is good as a therapeutic device for encouraging a positive sense of identity but its
   lack of program has prevented it from becoming a political strategy. The failure of black power is part of the whole failure of
   American radicalism which is trapped in the rhetoric and postures
   of the past.

Lewis, Claude. "The Black Caucus in Congress." Black Politician 3
   (July 1971): 13-17.

   Twelve black members of the U. S. House of Representatives
   formally organized and made public their intention to develop and
   use their political power to aid their constituencies.

Lightfoot, Claude. "The Right of Black America to Create a Black
   Nation." Political Affairs 47 (November 1968): 1-11.

   During the 1930s the Communist part was active in fostering integration, although it had passed a resolution calling for self-
   determination as a primary goal. At the 1959 convention this resolution was withdrawn, since northern migration had destroyed
   the territorial unity of the Black Belt. Paradoxically, there was

then a significant trend toward support of the Black Muslim movement. Currently there is a trend toward a program of separation
and the building of a black nation in the South.

Lomax, Louis. "When 'Nonviolence' Meets 'Black Power.'" In To Kill
a Black Man, pp. 113-97. Los Angeles: Holloway House, 1968.

Martin Luther King's first confrontation (in 1964) with the black
power movement in Mississippi is described. The second March
on Washington (which was later called the Poor People's March and
was held shortly after King's assassination) was planned as a show
of unity under King's banner, but by the time King went to Memphis
it was evident that the black power concept had superseded nonviolence as a mass movement.

McKissick, Floyd B. "Programs for Black Power." In The Black
Power Revolt, edited by Floyd B. Barbour, pp. 211-14. New York:
Collier, 1968.

The black power movement attempts to acquire power and control
for black Americans in the areas of politics, economics, federal
law enforcement, and consumer power; it also attempts to improve
the self-images of blacks. Programs must be developed to take
these needs beyond mere rhetoric. McKissick thinks that political
power will continue to be the most difficult to achieve because it
threatens the base of the white power structure.

McLemore, Leslie Burl. "Mississippi Freedom Democratic Party."
Black Politician 3 (October 1971): 19-22.

An analysis of third party theories as they apply to the Mississippi Freedom Democratic Party.

Muse, Benjamin. The American Negro Revolution: From Nonviolence
to Black Power, 1963-1967. Bloomington, Ind.: Indiana University Press, 1968.

In 1966 the civil rights movement under SCLC's leadership was
challenged by CORE and SNCC under the umbrella concept of black
power. CORE's actions were more constructive than the SNCC
approach under Stokely Carmichael. The phrase "black power"
stimulated interest in black history and culture, but it also resulted in the white backlash, which the civil rights movement was not
able to overcome.

"New Meaning for 'Black Power.'" Interview with Dr. Thomas W.
Matthew. U.S. News and World Report 65 (July 22, 1968): 32-33.

The National Economic Growth and Reconstruction Organization
(NEGRO) is described by its president, Dr. Thomas W. Matthew,

as a "national self-help program to build a people in pride, dignity, and self-respect through economic independence." Dr. Matthew argues that his movement is not separatist but a vehicle toward integration of the races.

Newton, Huey P. Revolutionary Suicide. New York: Harcourt Brace Jovanovich, 1973.

In his autobiography Newton describes the events and influences which led to the founding of the Black Panther party. The party was formed as a vehicle for political organization; its program evolved gradually. After Newton's release from prison in 1970, he eliminated the military trappings which set the Panthers apart from the black community. Newton implies that he intends to pursue more conventional political tactics.

Nolan, William A. Communism Versus the Negro. Chicago: Henry Regnery, 1951.

This anti-Communist case study includes an analysis of the Communist party's response to the American race problem since about 1920. Nolan describes the two dominant principles that the party applied to the American situation: self-determination in the Black Belt, and equal rights in the North. Self-determination received little support from blacks.

O'Dell, J. H. "The Contours of the 'Black Revolution' in the 1970's." Freedomways 10 (Second Quarter 1970): 104-14. *

Ottley, Herb. "Nation Time or Integration Time?" Black World 20 (July 1971): 41, 69-75.

A nationalist suggests that desire for political control of urban centers as put forth by Baraka is a distorted view of nationalist aims. Urban centers represent the failure of American capitalism. (Newark, one of the most depressed cities, is also one of the few with a strong black political organization.) Ottley asserts that black Americans must establish a powerful nation in Africa in order to have power in the U.S. equivalent to that of other immigrant groups such as Italians and Jews.

Pinkney, Alphonso. "The Assimilation of Afro-Americans." Black Scholar 1 (December 1969): 36-46.

Increasing numbers of black people are recognizing the fact that temporary autonomy, something short of permanent black separation, is the minimum acceptable solution to the racial crisis. The pluralist form of racial organization will enable black Americans to work for self-determination and to accumulate power.

Poinsett, Alex. "Roy Innis: Nation-Builder." Ebony 24 (October 1969): 170-76.

> Innis's role within CORE is described. The organization's three-part program for black liberation includes: Congressional passage of the Community Self-Determination Bill created by CORE; implementation of the theory that black people should control the institutions within their communities; and development of a new U.S. constitution which would deal with black and white people as two distinct groups. CORE's separatist doctrine means that black people would control their communities' economic and social services.

Record, Wilson. Race and Radicalism: The NAACP and the Communist Party in Conflict. Ithaca, N.Y.: Cornell University Press, 1964.

> Communism is linked to Garveyism and the Black Muslim movement in terms of the espousing of separatism as a solution to the race problem; the NAACP and newer direct-action groups have been integrationist. The party received its widest support from blacks when it emphasized legal redress of grievances, as in the Scottsboro case. This policy was an aberration from its central one, the advocacy of an all-black state in the Black Belt. A separate state was never culturally or psychologically feasible because the NAACP's integrationism represents the mainstream of social reform thought, while the Communist party is a radical movement with little long-term support.

Roberts, Gene. "Negro Nationalism a Black Power Key." New York Times, 24 July 1966, pp. 1, 51.

> This article takes the pulse of the civil rights movement after Stokely Carmichael's first use of the phrase "Black Power." Roy Innis's views are presented as representative of the new black nationalism. Innis calls for black power advocates to reject integration, to band themselves into a racially oriented mass movement, and to use political power and economic boycotts to win complete economic and political control of areas in which blacks are the numerical majority.

Roucek, Joseph S. "The Rise of 'Black Power' in the United States." Contemporary Review 212 (January 1968): 31-39.

> Traces black power and black nationalism to an angry and amorphous black community which is out of the American and American black mainstream. These movements will not effect progressive social change unless American politics is reorganized.

Rustin, Bayard. "Community Control: Separatism Repackaged." New York Times, 12 June 1972, p. 45.

The community control movement is a "spiritual descendant" of States' rights. The problems of racial integration are so complex that the clout of the federal government is needed to help solve them.

Salaam, Kalamu. "Floyd McKissick, Architect of Soul City, a Bold New Experiment in Living." Black Collegian 4 (March-April 1974): 32-33.

In this interview McKissick states that Soul City will serve black people by employing black professionals and technicians and by providing role models for black children.

Samuels, Gertrude. "Two Ways: Black Muslim and N.A.A.C.P." New York Times Magazine, 12 May 1963, pp. 26-27+.*

Smith, Edward C. "The Coming of the Black Ghetto-State." Yale Review 61 (Winter 1972): 161-82.

The ghetto is the first land the black man has owned and the black revolution would be an effort to control that land. The Community Action Agencies of the OEO helped give the black man his first taste of self-determination. The author illuminates the major historical factors of the black revolution.

Stone, Chuck. Black Political Power in America. Indianapolis: Bobbs-Merrill, 1968.

Black power is defined as political power. If the increasing number of black elected officials can demand and receive their proportionate share in decision-making, the economic problems of the black community will be solved. If white resistance prevents this, blacks will be forced to form a black third party. Both the black power movement and the white backlash tend to further separate the races.

Stone, Chuck. "The National Conference on Black Power." In The Black Power Revolt, edited by Floyd B. Barbour, pp. 189-98. Boston: Porter Sargent, 1968.

A report on the history and formation of the National Conference on Black Power in Newark, New Jersey, in July 1967. From 26 states and 126 cities, over 1,000 black people convened in fourteen workshops and passed the "Black Power Manifesto" which questions the value of integration and affirms the need for blacks to develop and govern their own institutions and programs.

Stone, Chuck. "Third Force, Third Party or Third-Class Influence?" Black Scholar 1 (December 1969): 8-13.

> Since we are now in an era of "white consensus politics" and since the differences between the two major political parties are minimal, Stone argues for the establishment of a Third Force or Liberation Party whose task would be to provide for blacks the political flexibility characteristic of white ethnic political power.

"They Think You're an Airplane and You're Really a Bird!" Interview with LeRoi Jones after the Newark riots. Evergreen Review 50 (December 1967): 51-53+.

> LeRoi Jones (Imamu Amiri Baraka) states that black people should be in control of all positions and resources in black communities. Newark will become an all-black city as whites flee to the suburbs and blacks organize political power. Spirit House, his community arts center, is available only to black audiences.

Turner, James. "The Sociology of Black Nationalism." Black Scholar 1 (December 1969): 18-27.

> A discussion of the sociological and historical background of the black nationalist movement as a springboard to defining it as a "conscious cultivation of social and cultural pluralism and a movement toward political self-determination."

Walton, Hanes, Jr. Black Political Parties—An Historical and Political Analysis. New York: Free Press, 1972.

> An analytic discussion of the development of black political parties before 1968. The black political party can be viewed as an independent party (an offshoot of a national multiracial one) or as a separate party, composed on a smaller level for a small community. Blacks have opted for each type of party at different times, but always with the direction and desire to enter the political system, not to overthrow it.

Walton, Hanes, Jr. Black Politics—A Theoretical and Structural Analysis. New York: Lippincott, 1972.

> A history of blacks' attempts to enter the political scene through the ballot. Blacks have been forced to use politics to gain the civil rights automatically granted to whites. Since 1957 black activists have brought about many improvements in federal laws on voting rights, thus ensuring blacks greater opportunity to enter the system and effect change.

Walton, Hanes, Jr. The Negro in Third Party Politics. Philadelphia: Dorrance, 1969.

> Black participation in the smaller third parties usually took place when their protest efforts were thwarted by the major parties. On the other hand, blacks did not hesitate to leave the third parties when it was opportune to use major parties to further civil rights for minority groups.

Walton, Hanes, Jr. The Political Philosophy of Martin Luther King, Jr. Westport, Conn.: Greenwood, 1971.

> A systematic examination of Martin Luther King's political philosophy. King was a political theologian, whose view of divine law transcended his own social and religious community. Consequently, King erred in extending his interpretation of divine law to all people and all situations. King's political thought was fragmentary and unsystematic, and was based on moral ideas converted into a political philosophy. Nevertheless, his philosophy was effective when applied to situations involving racial discrimination, although he placed too much reliance on nonviolence as a method.

Weaver, Robert C. Dilemmas of Urban America. Cambridge, Mass.: Harvard University Press, 1965.

> In the Godkin Lectures given at Harvard University in 1965, Weaver develops his belief that rigid approaches to housing problems will not be effective, although he also states that partnership between private enterprise and government is essential. While supporting the theory that new housing must be built in integrated settings, Weaver suggests the upgrading of existing housing in ghettos as part of the overall program.

Weaver, Robert C. "Housing Policy for Metropolitan Areas." Focus (Joint Center for Political Studies) 2 (December 1973): 4-6.

> Excerpts from testimony of the former Secretary of Housing and Urban Development before a subcommittee of the House Banking and Currency Committee. The major housing problem facing cities is the need to reverse the trend toward racial and economic stratification, and to provide some freedom of housing choice for lower-income families. Weaver recommends the establishment of metropolitan housing agencies to provide subsidized housing in cities and surrounding suburban areas, so that housing can be used as a means of desegregating suburbs and encouraging white families to remain in the cities.

Wilson, James Q. "The Negro in Politics." Daedalus 94 (Fall 1965): 949-73.

Wilson analyzes black voting patterns in the North and the South. He doubts that voting rights legislation will result in vastly improved living conditions for blacks. Wilson sees divisions among black leaders resulting not simply from ideology or personal rivalry, but from the effort to adapt the civil rights movement to incompatible (but pragmatically necessary) positions. The shifting alliances required by the American political system will divide the civil rights movement and limit its effectiveness. Because of the structure of American politics and the nature of the black community, black politics will accomplish only limited objectives. Wilson thinks that insubstantial gains may lead to an increase of nationalist sentiments.

Worthy, William. "An All-Black Party." Liberator 3 (October 1963): 18-19.

A call for support of the National Committee for a Freedom Now Party whose purpose would be to encourage black registration and voting and to serve as an advocate for black people's interests on local, state, and national issues.

Wright, Nathan, ed. What Black Politicians Are Saying. New York: Hawthorn, 1972.

Articles by Anna R. Langford, Mervyn M. Dymally, John Conyers, Kenneth A. Gibson, Percy Sutton, John Logan Cashin, and others discuss the problems and possibilities of political power to affect the status of black people. The importance of registering and voting is mentioned repeatedly as are the need for black organizations, black self-interest programs and new coalitions to help bring about social and economic advancement.

6. THE ECONOMIC ORDER: BLACK ENTERPRISE,
   BLACK WORKERS AND INCOME

Allen, Robert. Black Awakening in Capitalist America: An Analytic
   History. Garden City, N. Y.: Doubleday, 1969.*

Anderson, Jervis. A. Philip Randolph: A Biographical Portrait. New
   York: Harcourt Brace Jovanovich, 1973.

   This biography of Randolph includes descriptions of Randolph's
   work with Chandler Owen on The Messenger, as well as establishment of the Brotherhood of Sleeping Car Porters. A strain of nationalism runs through Randolph's religious and social heritage;
   nationalism and separatism could well have become the central
   principle in his philosophy, but it did not.

Anderson, Talmadge. "Black Economic Liberation Under Capitalism."
   Black Scholar 2 (October 1970): 10-14.

   Tokenism and psuedointegration are tools used by the capitalist
   system to exploit blacks. Anderson thinks that a strong, separate
   black capitalist economy will lead blacks to liberation because
   power respects power.

Association of Black Social Workers. "Code of Ethics." Black Caucus
   3 (Fall 1970).

   "If a sense of community awareness is a precondition to humani-
   tarian acts, then we as social workers must look to our skills and
   commitment and translate that into concrete benefits to the Black
   community. We will serve mankind best by serving our own people first. When we address our expertise to the quality of life of
   Black people in America, the appropriate roles for us must be
   guided by Black consciousness and advocacy in addressing the security and needs of the Black community."

Bates, Timothy. "The Potential of Black Capitalism." Public Policy
   22 (Winter 1973): 135-48.

   To support his belief that the erosion of segregation will yield
   great opportunities for black entrepreneurs, Bates analyzes

responses to recent federal programs for making long-term credit available.

Blackman, Courtney. Black Capitalism in Economic Perspective. New York: Irving Trust Company, 1973.

Black capitalism holds a limited but useful function in black economic development. Its psychological contribution will be much greater than its financial contribution. Visible black business can provide the cutting edge of the black drive toward significant economic power.

Bonds, Ozell, Jr. "The Case for Independent Black Trade Unions." Ebony 26 (August 1970): 142-44.

Full black participation in the trade unions will occur only after independent black-controlled trade unions are established.

Brazeal, Brailsford R. The Brotherhood of Sleeping Car Porters: Its Origin and Development. New York: Harper, 1946.

An account of the establishment and development of the first successful black union. Black workers must depend more on favorable labor legislation than on strikes, unless they are able to integrate those unions which have been traditionally white. An integrated labor movement should be the goal, but separate unions must be used as a stopgap measure.

Brimmer, Andrew F. "The Black Revolution and the Economic Future of Negroes in the United States." American Scholar 38 (Autumn 1969): 629-43.*

Brimmer, Andrew F. "Economic Developments in the Black Community." Public Interest 34 (Winter 1974): 146-63.

An examination of the impact of Great Society programs of the 1960s on the black worker. Analysis of the effects of several manpower programs indicates that most participants derived measurable gains from the programs. Nevertheless, the net impact of manpower programs and occupational upgrading was less than optimal. Black capitalism as promoted in the first Nixon Administration was a total failure, although the absence of quantifiable evidence limits Brimmer's certainty. Black-owned businesses face extraordinary risks because of the lack of equity capital, low level of managerial skills, and lack of diversification into high-growth industries.

Brimmer, Andrew F. "Economic Integration and the Progress of the Negro Community." Ebony 26 (August 1970): 118-21.

Separatism and black capitalism are dismissed as illusions rather than as viable alternatives.

Brimmer, Andrew F. "Negroes in an Integrated Society." Public Relations Journal 24 (July 1968): 19.

Blacks will be able to influence political decisions in cities when they vote as a bloc. On the other hand, the prospects for a viable all-black economy are not promising. Most blacks will have to be employed in large national industries which will not concentrate their plants in the ghetto. Negro-owned business will not be able to employ all blacks needing jobs, nor will they be able to serve only blacks.

Brimmer, Andrew F., and Terrel, Henry S. "The Economic Potential of Black Capitalism." Black Politician 2 (April 1971): 19-23+.

An analysis of the economic potential of black capitalism, with the reasons for the authors' disenchantment with that strategy as a means of black economic development.

Brooke, Edward W. "Minority Enterprise—The Need for Bold Initiatives and Staunch Allies." Speech to the Contractors' Association of Boston, 2 March 1974.

Blacks need bold strategies to gain control of the gross national product of the black community. Dollars should be kept in the black community to create new jobs, to make services accessible to the poor, and to create a sense of community pride. The role of black politicians is to see that blacks have the opportunity to acquire economic power.

Brooke, Edward W. Speech to the Third Annual Dinner of the Congressional Black Caucus. Washington, D. C., 29 September 1973. *

Brooks, Thomas R. "Workers, Black and White: DRUMbeats in Detroit." Dissent 17 (January-February 1970): 16-31.

Description of the origin of DRUM (Dodge Revolutionary Union Movement) from within the ranks of black auto-industry workers. DRUM, the founding contingent of the League of Revolutionary Black Workers, agitates for more black leadership and control in the union and the auto plants.

Browne, Robert S. "Economic Case for Reparations to Black America." American Economic Review 62 (May 1972): 39-46.

Browne outlines America's failure to rectify its treatment of blacks. Reparations must be discussed within its moral and political context. The question relates to the issue of redistribution of wealth. The author suggests several methods which could be used to compute a reasonable reparations figure; and makes several suggestions for implementation of a reparations payment.

Bunche, Ralph J. "A Critical Analysis of the Tactics and Programs of Minority Groups." Journal of Negro Education 4 (July 1935): 308-20.*

DuBois, W. E. B. Dusk of Dawn: An Essay Toward an Autobiography of a Race Concept. New York: Harcourt, 1940.*

DuBois, W. E. B. "Segregation." Crisis 41 (January 1934): 10.

In order for the black masses to advance, it is necessary to establish a black cooperative economy. Segregation does not necessarily mean discrimination; the policies of the NAACP were directed, not against separation, but against discrimination. DuBois writes, "It [NAACP] has never denied the recurrent necessity of united separate action on the part of Negroes for self-defense and self-development."

Henderson, Vivian W. Text of Address for Plans of Progress College Relations Conference. Atlanta, April 29, 1968.*

Hobson, Julius. "Black Power: Right or Left?" In The Black Power Revolt, edited by Floyd B. Barbour, pp. 238-43. New York: Collier, 1968.

Advocates of black power must decide whether to build black capitalism, which could be as exploitative and racist as the existing capitalist system, or whether to internationalize the struggle and move toward a world economic system. Hobson favors the latter idea.

Hopps, June G. "A Planning Model for Black Community Development." Review of Black Political Economy 4 (Winter 1974): 57-73.

The poverty programs of the 1960s did not change the basic conditions of economic life for the majority of the black population. Blacks must devise strategies for community development which rely on the communities' own resources, and avoid the debilitating consequences of national policy shifts.

Innis, Roy. "Separatist Economics: A New Social Contract." In Black Economic Development, by The American Assembly, Columbia University, pp. 50-59. Englewood Cliffs, N. J.: Prentice-Hall, 1969.

Innis defines separatist economics as ". . . manipulation of the economy of black areas in a preferential way to obtain an edge and protect the interests of the [black] community; to place a membrane around the community that allows full commercial intercourse with outside business interests while setting preconditions and guidelines advantageous to the community . . . ."

Innis, Roy, and Hill, Norman. "Black Self-Determination: A Debate." New Generation 51 (Summer 1969): 18-26.

Innis describes CORE's plan for creating viable black economic bases in ghettos, as a move toward establishing community corporations in black areas which will coordinate economic development and community services. He emphasizes that the Community Self-Development Act, as it is called, is pragmatic rather than ideological. Norman Hill of the A. Philip Randolph Institute sees separatism, self-determination, and community control as black defenses to white Americans' failure to provide the economic security that is the basis for social justice and political freedom.

Jackson, Jesse L. "Confronting Monopoly and Keeping the Movement Moving." Freedomways 14 (First Quarter 1974): 7-14.

Unemployment and inflation are causing a deterioration in living standards, thereby disproving the myth that each generation's living standard and opportunity improve. The energy crisis hoax affects blacks by making the achievement of full employment even more difficult. "The greatest waste of energy is the waste of human lives, resulting from poor education, unemployment, and the limiting of opportunity."

Jackson, Jesse L. "Three Challenges to Organized Labor." Freedomways 12 (Fourth Quarter 1972): 307-15.

Based on the keynote address delivered to the convention of the Amalgamated Cutters and Butchers' Workmen of North America, AFL-CIO, in Florida, August 9, 1972. The three challenges are: labor must use its power to make economic rights the first priority on the nation's human rights agenda; labor must win back the support of blue collar workers who decided that human rights and law and order are incompatible; labor must see that black voter registration is increased. Jackson also describes the activities of Operation P. U. S. H.

Jacobson, Julius, ed. The Negro and the American Labor Movement. Garden City, N. Y.: Anchor, 1968.

This anthology includes original essays. Most writers emphasize discrimination from conservative unions. Several provide a historical summary of events and trends from the Civil War to 1955.

"Jesse Jackson and Operation Breadbasket: In Search of a New Alternative." Black Enterprise 1 (May 1970): 18-23.

Operation Breadbasket was started by Jesse Jackson to monitor large chain stores operating in the black community. The goals of Breadbasket are to end discriminatory hiring and promoting practices, as well as to bolster black-owned businesses and black capitalism by means of boycotts and picketing.

Killens, John O. "Black Labor and the Black Liberation Movement." Black Scholar 2 (October 1970): 33-39.

Although there has been progress in the black liberation struggles, black labor, the real potential power, has not been tapped. Black labor is still controlled by white leadership, and white leadership has never been interested in the liberation of blacks. A "National Black Labor Congress" is needed to organize and direct black labor to spearhead the struggle against the exploiters of all black people.

McLauren, Dunbar S. "Short-range Separatism." Ebony 26 (August 1970): 123.

The purpose of black capitalism or black economic development is to lead blacks to leberation. Separatism in business is a stage toward economic equality of black and white America.

Marshall, Kenneth E. "Ghetto Economic Development." Black Caucus 1 (Fall 1968): 22-26.

Marshall thinks that there is no contradiction between working for the end of the ghetto while at the same time seeking economic development of present ghetto residents. Their improved skills and attitudes, by-products of a program of ghetto redevelopment, are prerequisites for an open society. He does not believe that the more sophisticated advocates of black power envision a separate and viable black America, but rather are more aware than earlier civil rights leaders of the process by which the goals of equality will be achieved.

Marshall, Ray. The Negro and Organized Labor. New York: Wiley, 1965.

This analysis of discrimination by unions states that organized labor should create a framework within which blacks can overcome historical handicaps. Education and training for all low-income groups would best help blacks to fit into the numerous existing hiring programs. The black-labor alliance will be of increasing political importance, particularly in the South.

Ofari, Earl. The Myth of Black Capitalism. New York: Monthly Review Press, 1970.

Cooperation between the black elite, the white corporate world, and the federal government has begun to yield a few black-owned businesses. However, the community development corporations set up by the Small Business Administration will be controlled by white business interests, not by the black community. The government and white business will not allow blacks to control capital; the failure of the effort to establish black capitalism will encourage solidarity in the black community. Before blacks can acquire political power, capitalism—the instrument of their oppression—must be destroyed.

"Playboy Interview: Jesse Jackson." Playboy (November 1969): 85+.

Jesse Jackson discusses the rationale and program of Operation Breadbasket, a self-help organization whose primary goals are to create jobs for blacks and to encourage blacks to own and operate businesses. He describes Operation Breadbasket's most potent weapon, the boycott, and its effectiveness against the Atlantic and Pacific Tea Company's stores in Chicago's black ghetto.

Roberts, Gene. "Negro Nationalism a Black Power Key." New York Times, 24 July 1966, pp. 1, 51.*

Rustin, Bayard. "The Failure of Black Separatism." Harper's 240 (January 1970): 25-32.*

Schlesinger, Stephen C. "Black Caucus in the Unions." Nation 218 (February 2, 1974): 142-44.

One year after its formation, the Coalition of Black Trade unionists included thirty-three unions representing one million black workers. The coalition's officers see its purpose as reducing black unemployment and integrating the still largely segregated unions, such as the building trades. Schlesinger calls the coalitions' actions interest-group liberalism.

Seder, John, and Burrell, Berkeley G. Getting It Together: Black
   Businessmen in America. New York: Harcourt Brace Jovanovich,
   1971.

   These case histories of successful black businessmen show that black
   enterprises tend to be small retail and service establishments.
   White business and the government have done little to help black entrepreneurs; black capitalism will solve many of the ghetto's economic ills.

"Segregated Professional Association?" Social Service Review 41 (December 1967): 435.

   The creation of the Association of Black Social Workers.

Spero, Sterling D. , and Harris, Abram L. The Black Worker: The
   Negro and the Labor Movement. New York: Columbia University
   Press, 1931.

   An attempt to describe and analyze the results of a study of the
   relation of black workers to the labor movement. Independent
   black unions which have arisen in occupations with substantial
   black members must accept standards set by the dominant white
   groups, and are dependent upon white unions' support in negotia-
   tions. The authors suspect that all-black unions will develop
   strong leaders who will be able to break down barriers in the other
   labor movements.

Sturdivant, Frederick D. "The Limits of Black Capitalism." Harvard
   Business Review 47 (January-February 1969): 122-28.

   A professor of business at the University of Texas describes the
   Community Self-Determination Bill introduced in the U. S. Senate
   in July, 1968. The legislation would create community-owned development corporations, established to gain ownership and control
   of the economic resources of their communities. The bill was
   drafted in the spirit of black separatism, and its enactment would
   retard the necessary economic revolution in the ghetto.

Tyler, Lawrence L. "The Protestant Ethic Among the Black Muslims."
   Phylon 27 (Spring 1966): 5-14.

   An analysis of the historical and social relationship between the
   Protestant ethic and capitalism. The religious ethic of the Black
   Muslims qualifies as a form of asceticism and, as such, parallels
   Weber's Protestant ethic theory. This ethic greatly facilitated
   the economic inequality of lower-class blacks, the very ones who
   are attracted to the Black Muslim cult. As in Protestantism, the
   Muslims will eventually be secularized by the drive for

accumulating capital and this will have a degenerative effect on their values and creed.

Walton, Sidney. "Geographic Proposals for Black Economic Liberation." Black Scholar 3 (February 1972): 38-47.

Programs such as black capitalism and manpower training have failed to improve the economic status of most blacks. Walton thinks the key to black economic deprivation is that blacks lack freedom of economic mobility. As a solution, he proposes implementation of an economic integration program to encourage out-migration from ghetto areas. The federal government should induce geographic mobility by regionally setting up and coordinating industrial relocation and by funding planned black migration.

Wright, Robert E. "Black Capitalism: Toward Controlled Development of Black America." Negro Digest 19 (December 1969): 27-33.

Black capitalism, here defined as the collective accumulation of capital (land and material resources) for the benefit of all black people, is in opposition to western monopoly capitalism. This definition of black capitalism is tied in with cultural revolution, and must oppose integration and "class struggle" politics.

7. RELIGION AND RACE: CHURCH STRUCTURES
AND REDRESSING INEQUITIES

Becker, William H. "Black Power in Christological Perspective."
Religion in Life 38 (Autumn 1969): 404-14.

Analyzes two Christian models of behavior, the passive, suffering
model and the rebellious model. The rebel is more evident in the
racial crisis, particularly in the black power movement. Martin
Luther King's approach was rebellious in comparison to the passivity which preceded it, but the stance of more militant rebels
caused King to appear to be a passive sufferer. The two models
are inseparable, both in theology and in social application. Thus,
advocates of both black power and nonviolence are equally within
the Christian tradition.

Berrigan, Philip. No More Strangers. New York: Macmillan, 1965.

Three of the essays in this volume are concerned with race problems and the church. Berrigan attacks the hypocrisy of the
Christian church for its failure to challenge segregation. He sees
nationalism as a desperate response to the failure of other methods.

Brotz, Howard. The Black Jews of Harlem. New York: Schocken,
1964.

The first part of this book concerns a religious group whose members claim to be Jews and who deny any ethnic or racial affiliation
to another group they describe as "so-called Negroes." The second part of the book is devoted to the various forms of nationalism
among blacks in the United States.

Browne, Robert S. "Economic Case for Reparations to Black America." American Economic Review 62 (May 1972): 39-46.*

Browne, Robert S. "Toward Making 'Black Power' Real Power." In
Black Manifesto: Religion, Racism, and Reparations, edited by
Robert S. Lecky and H. Elliott Wright, pp. 65-77. New York:
Sheed and Ward, 1969.

An analysis of ways in which our society can come to grips with the inequality of wealth between blacks and whites. Browne supports the demands made by the Black Manifesto because it is one of the levers necessary to extract resources for the black community.

Burns, W. Haywood. "Black Muslims in America: A Reinterpretation." Race 5 (July 1963): 26-37.

In spite of its racist indictment of white power, the Black Muslim movement is not violently aggressive. And while on the surface it rejects America, its values—cleanliness, education, hard work, and discipline—are predominantly middle-class. The Black Muslim movement has provided many blacks with a new identity and a means through which to vent their anger.

Chamberlain, Gary L. "Has 'Benign Neglect' Invaded the Churches?" Christian Century 9 (April 24, 1974): 448-51.

Most Protestant denominations denounced the Black Manifesto and its promotors' tactics, but responded anyway with increased funding for urban and race-related programs. Chamberlain says that these economic programs must be paired with educational programs to combat racism in local congregations. The Black Manifesto has helped to bring about some social change, and the black caucuses have served a particularly useful function by providing a focus for minority voices, by involving minorities in decision-making processes, by helping to establish a black theology, and by checking the paternalism evident in the social programs of the church.

Clark, Kenneth B. Letter to Homer A. Jack, November 2, 1967.

A statement rejecting the rationale and methodology of a black separatist movement within the Unitarian Universalist Association on the grounds that racial separatist demands by human beings with darker skins are as insidious as similar demands by human beings with light skins.

Cleage, Albert. The Black Messiah. New York: Sheed and Ward, 1968.

The black church has always been an integral part of black communities, but it has failed to instill in its members a sense of power and control over their own lives. This collection of sermons by the pastor of the Shrine of the Madonna in Detroit is meant to serve as the basis for a theology that uses power and religious ritual to encourage political action and economic independence in black communities.

Dowey, Edward A., Jr. "'The Black Manifesto': Revolution, Reparation, Separation." Theology Today 26 (October 1969): 288-93.

The aim of the Black Manifesto was to give blacks encouragement
to seek a measure of economic control. It is separatist in that it
recognizes the failure of the integration movement. The terms of
the Black Manifesto can only solidify white resistance, which in
turn will reinforce black dissatisfactions with liberalism.

DuBois, W. E. B. "Will the Church Remove the Color Line?" Chris-
tian Century 48 (December 9, 1931): 1554-6. Reprinted in W. E. B.
DuBois: A Reader, edited by Meyer Weinberg, pp. 219-26. New
York: Harper and Row, 1970.

After capsuling attempts of certain white American churches to ex-
pel black members, DuBois concludes that white churches will
continue to side with wealth and power. They will support segregation for as long as possible, but will defend integration in Christian terms once it has occurred.

"Elijah Muhammad." In The Negro Since Emancipation, edited by
Harvey Wish, pp. 170-82. Englewood Cliffs, N. J.: Prentice-Hall,
1964.

Following a brief introduction, the selections included here are
from Elijah Muhammad's writings in Muhammad Speaks. His addresses of March 13 and March 28, 1964, suggest a separate state
for blacks. Discussed also are separation of the races, pacifism,
Martin Luther King and the civil rights movement, and his disagreement with the latter. The Black Muslim program is summar-
ized here also.

Epps, Archie. "A Negro Separatist Movement of the Nineteenth Century." Harvard Review 4 (Summer 1969): 69-87. *

Essien-Udom, E. U. Black Nationalism: The Search for an Identity in
America. Chicago: University of Chicago Press, 1962. *

Fichter, Joseph H. "American Religion and the Negro." Daedalus 94
(Fall 1965): 1085-1106.

Black religious and nationalist movements (Garveyism, Black Muslims) dramatize the plight of blacks in America. They also serve
the function of arousing white Americans to the needs for justice
and integration. The fundamentalist and Pentecostal groups which
are not interested in the civil rights movement are characterized
as escapist. The large Christian and Jewish denominations have
been instrumental in eliminating racial discrimination.

Forman, James. The Making of Black Revolutionaries. New York: Macmillan, 1972.

   Forman has been the primary force behind the reparations move-
   ment. In his autobiography, he describes his work in the National
   Black Economic Conference and the Interreligious Foundation for
   Community Organization, and includes his reflections on his dis-
   ruption of the service at Riverside Church in New York City on
   May 4, 1969.

Fraser, C. Gerald. "Separatism Path Urged for Blacks." New York
   Times, 15 November 1972, p. 43.

   During the question-and-answer period of the first session of the
   1972-73 Institute of Religious Studies at Jewish Theological Seminary, two theologians—a Protestant and a Jew—Dr. Deborah
   Partridge Wolfe and Rabbi David Luber recommend that black
   Americans develop their own black institutions as a means of ac-
   quiring self-identity, group cohesiveness and strength.

Frazier, E. Franklin. The Negro Church in America. New York:
   Schocken, 1963.

   This posthumously published volume includes Frazier's perspective on the religion of the slaves, freedmen's churches, the psychological function of religion, and the black church as a social
   institution. Frazier blames the authoritarianism and domination
   of the black church for the slowness of blacks to become integrated
   into white society. He expects that black churches will disinte-
   grate as segregation disappears.

Harding, Vincent. "Black Power and the American Christ." Christian Century 84 (January 4, 1967): 10-13.

   Blacks have begun to repudiate the American Christ as a symbol
   of white racism and hypocrisy. Black power is a rejection of
   American culture and religion and a search for a religious reality
   that speaks to blacks. Harding hopes that black power becomes
   the means by which blacks pull themselves out of their mourning
   and nostalgia for the days of glory in the civil rights movement.

Harrington, Donald Szantho. "Sin, Separatism, Solidarity and the
   Future of Race Relations." New York: Community Church of New
   York, 1970.

   In this sermon the author explains his reasons for feeling that the
   "frankly separatist outlook" of the Black Unitarian Universalist
   Caucus is a mistake. "Sin," according to Paul Tillich, "is separation . . . ." Furthermore, separation will only increase white

racism and discrimination. Harrington supports the black and white action group working to support racial integration.

Hough, Joseph C. Black Power and White Protestants: A Christian Response to the New Negro Pluralism. New York: Oxford University Press, 1968.

To counteract the fear and misunderstanding about black power among white Americans, the author places the phenomenon in the perspective of American race relations as it has evolved and changed since World War II. The phenomenon, he writes, represents a change in Negro strategy for social justice and a rise in ethnocentrism. He urges white Protestants to seek new patterns of response to black power by shifting emphasis from integrated churches.

Howlett, Duncan. "A Unitarian Universalist Response to the Black Rebellion." Sermon delivered at All Souls Church Unitarian, October 15, 1967, Washington, D. C.

The author voices grave concern about the Black Caucus formed at the conference on Unitarian Universalist Response to the Black Rebellion. He asks, "Are we now to repudiate the ideal [of brotherhood] and build racial distinctions into our denominational structure?"

Jack, Homer A. "Black Power Confronts Unitarian Universalists." Christian Century 85 (June 26, 1968): 849-50.

Outlines the development of a black nationalist consciousness in the Unitarian Universalist Association. At the 7th General Assembly in May 1964, most black delegates participated in the black caucus which presented demands to the organization. Jack points out that the controversy forced the organization to examine priorities. If genuine, their commitment to the amelioration of the urgent problem of race relations must be reflected in program and budget. He, along with other whites, will no longer speak for blacks, who have now taken the power to speak for the entire Unitarian Universalist denomination on the issue of race.

Jones, Miles J. "Why a Black Seminary?" Christian Century 89 (February 2, 1972): 124, 132-33.

The black seminary is needed by blacks "for the articulate interpretation of the experience through which we pass day after day"— that of sorrow and rejection, deprivation and depersonalization. A white seminary cannot use the daily experience of blacks to point out a meaningful theology.

Krosney, Herbert. "America's Black Supremacists." Nation 192 (May 6, 1961): 390-92.

A brief description of the history, beliefs, and religious practices of the Black Muslims.

Lecky, Robert S., and Wright, H. Elliot, eds. Black Manifesto: Religion, Racism, and Reparations. New York: Sheed and Ward, 1969.

Included are articles by James Forman, William Stringfellow, Robert S. Browne, and others that provide both an account of the development and presentation of the Black Manifesto and a multi-faceted analysis of the implications of the controversy.

Lincoln, C. Eric. The Black Muslims in America. Boston: Beacon, 1961.

A study of the Black Muslim movement in the United States which provides a description of the sect and also background and analysis of the concepts which give this pseudo-Islamic sect meaning and momentum.

Lomax, Louis. When the Word Is Given. Cleveland: World Publishing, 1963.

A popularized account of the Black Muslim movement based on newspaper articles and interviews with Black Muslims. Some discussion of the Muslims' demand for a separate black state and the dilemma they face by denouncing integration.

Marshall, Calvin B. "The Black Church—Its Mission Is Liberation." Black Scholar 2 (December 1970): 13-19.

Marshall sees four factors working against the black church as a strong force for liberation: the Afro-Saxon mind (desire to be white); the syndrome of the colonized (self-hate); slave mentality; and super-militancy.

Marx, Gary T. "Religion: Opiate or Inspiration of Civil Rights Militance Among Negroes?" American Sociological Review 32 (February 1967): 64-72.

A report on the results of a nationwide survey of religious involvement among blacks, which indicated that those blacks with the strongest religious involvement had the least militant attitudes on civil rights. Historically, the church in America has opposed fundamental social change because of potential jeopardy to its status. As the civil rights movement developed, it became evident that religion inhibited the growth of militance.

Morsell, John A. "The NAACP and 'Reparations.'" Crisis 77 (March 1970): 93-95, 101.

> A review of the NAACP's rejection of the issue of reparations as embodied in the "Black Manifesto" demands made upon American churches by James Forman; and a critical analysis of denominational activities spawned by the reparations issue.

National Committee of Negro Churchmen. "Black Power." New York Times, 31 July 1966, p. E5.

> An address to four groups of people for whom clarification of the meaning of black power seemed to be urgent: the leaders of America, white churchmen, the black community, and the press. The main theme is that the current controversy over the meaning and application of black power is based on the balance of power held by whites and sought by blacks. The address seeks to temper the fears of each group by recalling the true meaning of a democratic society and the common destiny of blacks and whites.

"Now Hear the Message of the Black Muslims from Their Leader, Elijah Muhammad." Esquire (April 1963): 97-101.

> A pictorial essay.

Parker, Robert A. The Incredible Messiah; The Deification of Father Divine. Boston: Little, Brown, 1937.

> This biography of Father Divine describes his cult and his social programs, which included the purchase of farms where ghetto dwellers could relocate. Father Divine is analyzed as a messianic figure. The rise of messianic movements correlates with social injustice and racial prejudice.

Payne, Daniel A. History of the African Methodist Episcopal Church. Nashville: Publishing House of the A. M. E. Sunday School Union, 1891.

> The creation of the A. M. E. Church from the Methodist Episcopal Church was necessary to give the black ministers independence of action and thought and a sense of responsibility for their own destiny.

Poinsett, Alex. "Black Revolt in White Churches." Ebony 23 (September 1968): 63-68.

> Black caucuses were formed as a response to the hypocrisy and racism in white Christian churches. Poinsett discusses different factions of the movement to restore Christianity as a viable institution for blacks.

Poole, Elijah (Elijah Muhammad). Message to the Black Man in America. Chicago: Muhammad Mosque of Islam No. 2, 1965.

A section of this book is a plea for racial separatism.

"Racist Church? Black Clergy Conference. " Commonweal 88 (May 10,
1968): 222.

There is only token black presence within the Catholic Church, and
members of the Black Clergy Conference called the Catholic Church
in the U. S. "a white racist institution" and demanded that there be
black priests on the diocesan level and, above all, in the black
community.

Ranck, Lee. "'I Want to Use Your Blackness.'" Engage/Social Action
2 (March 1974): 14-27.

Describes the United Methodist National Convocation on the Black
Church, a black caucus within the predominatly white United Methodist Church. The convocation was formed as a replacement for
the segregated Central Jurisdiction which had provided blacks an
opportunity to work together and which they lost when it was eliminated. Speakers emphasized the need for communication and cooperation among black Methodist congregations. Ranck states that
the few whites at the convocation must have realized their inability
to empathize with the experiences of black people in white America.

Reimers, David M. White Protestantism and the Negro. New York:
Oxford University Press, 1965.

This monograph, a history of the attitudes of white Protestants
toward segregation and civil rights, describes southern churches
which defended slavery, abolitionism, and Protestantism, and the
development of segregation in southern churches by the end of Reconstruction. Early twentieth-century revivalism was sometimes
sensitive to the civil rights issue. Reimers believes that the 1950s
saw the beginning of the trend toward condemning segregation as
unchristian, although there was little mass support for this position until the early 1960s.

Relyea, Harold C. "The Theology of Black Power. " Religion in Life
38 (Autumn 1969): 415-20.

Changing views of blackness within the black church parallel social thought. The theology of black power, as preached by Marcus
Garvey, Elijah Muhammad, and Detroit's Black Christian Nationalist Movement, includes a black God and a black Christ, who
provide a positive statement of racial pride and identity.

Reynolds, L. H. "Why Negro Churches Are a Necessity." A. M. E. Church Review (October 1887): 154-57.

This article, written by a layman, defends religious separatism on the grounds that there are differences between nationalities and races. One must recognize these differences and adjust one's relationships to avoid friction. "Therefore . . . the true course is for each race to have its separate churches to the intent of, as nearly as possible, reaching all; in order also to avoid such friction as arises from a co-mingling of the races before they are fully prepared for it . . . ."

Roberts, J. Deotis. "Black Theological Education: Programming for Liberation." Christian Century 91 (February 6, 1974): 117-18.

The author states that black liberation is one fashionable cause among many in white seminaries, but that the black seminary can devote its full energies to training ministers who will focus on social problems as they affect blacks. Pastoral field programs might be directed toward involvement beyond the parish, thus enabling the black church to fulfill its potential as the most important institution in black liberation.

Samuels, Gertrude. "Feud Within the Black Muslims." New York Times Magazine, 22 March 1964, pp. 17+.

A discussion of the split between Malcolm X and Elijah Muhammad and of the creation of Malcolm X's own party. The three elements that distinguish his new party from the old group are: (1) personal independence that will allow him to be master of his own house; (2) self-defense units; and (3) nationalist appeal to all blacks that allows cooperation with the interracial civil rights movement.

Samuels, Gertrude. "Two Ways: Black Muslim and N. A. A. C. P." New York Times Magazine, 12 May 1963, pp. 26-27+.

The nation's blacks are united in their desire for equality, but they are divided on the means to achieve it. Two diametrically opposed approaches are discussed here: the moderate integration tactics of the NAACP, and the Black Muslims' doctrine of black supremacy and the creation of a black state.

Schuchter, Arnold. Reparations: Black Manifesto and Its Challenge to White America. Philadelphia: Lippincott, 1970.

This book includes a detailed description of the controversy surrounding demands by James Forman and other black militants and churchmen for $150,000,000 for community programs as partial repayment for injustices against blacks as a result of racism.

Beginning in May 1969, these activists disrupted services at a number of churches; the disruption tactics were used after persuasion and many meetings had failed. Schuchter does not discuss the effect the Black Manifesto made on the subsequent social policy of the National Council of Churches.

Sleeper, Charles Freeman. Black Power and Christian Responsibility: Some Biblical Foundations for Social Ethics. Nashville: Abingdon, 1969.

The goal of black power is to strengthen black institutions; its strategy is independence rather than coalition. There is ambiguity in whether integration or separation is the goal, but most spokesmen think that equality must be attained through separatism. White congregations might use white power to create a favorable climate of public opinion, to encourage open housing, equal employment, and educational opportunity.

Tyler, Lawrence L. "The Protestant Ethic Among the Black Muslims." Phylon 27 (Spring 1966): 5-14. *

Wilmore, Gayraud S. "The Case for a New Black Church Style." In The Black Church in America, edited by Hart M. Nelson, Raytha L. Yokley and Anne K. Nelson, pp. 324-34. New York: Basic, 1971.

At the time of writing, Wilmore was an official in the United Presbyterian Church. He thinks that the strategy for solving the problems of black congregations in white society lies in immersion in black culture and the ideology of black power.

Wright, Nathan. Black Power and Urban Unrest: Creative Possibilities. New York: Hawthorn, 1967.

Wright, an Episcopal minister, was a member of the National Committee of Negro Churchmen which placed an advertisement titled "Black Power" in the New York Times of July 31, 1966. This statement appears as an appendix to Wright's essays on aspects of black power. The slogan "Black Power," defined to exclude separatist connotations, is used here as a symbol of blacks' potential contribution to a pluralistic American society.

name index

A & P. See Atlantic and Pacific Tea Co.

A. Philip Randolph Institute, 113

Abram, Morris, 71

AFL-CIO. See American Federation of Labor-Congress of Industrial Organizations

Africa, 4, 7, 8, 9, 10, 11, 13, 15, 16, 20, 21, 31, 32, 35, 36, 55

African Methodist Episcopal Church, 4, 124

African Studies and Research Center, Cornell University, 92

Africans, 5, 16, 42, 55, 58

Afro-American Society, Wesleyan University, 74

Afro-American Studies Dept., Harvard University, 80, 82, 85

Afro-American Studies Institute, Antioch College, 75, 86

Afro-American Studio for Acting and Speech, 52

Alabama, 32

Alabama Negro Colony, 14, 30

Albany Convention of Colored Citizens (1840), 8

All-University Summer Conference, Syracuse University, 64

Allen, Robert, 3

Alsop, Joseph, 59, 68

Amalgamated Cutters and Butchers Workmen of North America, AFL-CIO, 113

A. M. E. Church. See African Methodist Episcopal Church

American Colonization Society, 5, 9

American Council on Education, 87

American Federation of Labor-Congress of Industrial Organizations, 96

American Library Association, 95

American Negro Historical Association, 90

American Political Science Association, 100, 101

Anderson, Arthur A., 8

Anderson, Jervis, 109

128

Anderson, S. E. , 17

Anderson, Talmadge, 109

Anthony, Earl, 71

Antioch College, 86, 87; see also
    Afro-American Studies Institute

Aptheker, Herbert, 3

Association for the Study of Negro
    Life and History, 90

Association of Black Social Work-
    ers, 109, 116

Atlantic and Pacific Tea Co. , 115

Axam, John A. , 95

Baldwin, James, 17, 42, 52

Ballard, Allen B. , 71

Baraka, Amiri, xxiv, 18, 42, 63
    95, 103, 106

Barbaro, Fred, 59

Barbour, Floyd B. , 96

Baskin, Darryl, 18

Bates, Timothy, 109

Becker, William H. , 118

Beckham, Edgar F. , 71

Bell, Daniel, 72

Bell, Derrick, 59

Bell, Howard H. , 3

Berrigan, Philip, 118

Bennett, Lerone, Jr. , 19, 42

Billings, Charles E. , 19

Birenbaum, William, 64

Bittle, William E. , 8

Black, Algernon D. , 32

Black Christian Nationalist
    Movement, 125

Black Clergy Conference, 125

Black Legion, 30

Black Manifesto, 119, 120, 123,
    124, 127

Black Muslims, xxii, 17, 25, 28,
    32, 35, 39, 52, 56, 102, 104,
    116, 119, 120, 123, 124, 126

Black Panther Party, 4, 98, 103

Black Political Convention (1972),
    95

Black Power Manifesto, 105

Black Student Alliance, Yale
    University, 89

Black Unitarian Universalist
    Caucus, 121

Blake, J. Herman, 3, 73

Blackman, Courtney, 110

Blassingame, John W. , 73

Boggs, Grace, 96

Boggs, James, 96

Bolner, James, 60

Bond, Julian, 96

Bonds, Ozell, Jr., 110

Bone, Robert A., 43

Borders, William, 74

Borghese, Elizabeth Mann, 19

Boulding, Kenneth, 73

Boyd, Willis Dolmond, 8

Bracey, John H., 4

Brandeis University, 71

Brawley, Benjamin, 43

Brazeal, Brailsford R., 110

Breitman, George, 20

Briggs, Albert A., 60

Brimmer, Andrew F., 74, 86, 110, 111

Broderick, Francis L., 9

Brooke, Edward W., 74, 97, 111

Brooks, Thomas R., 111

Brotherhood of Sleeping Car Porters, 109

Brotz, Howard, 118

Brown et al. v. Board of Education of Topeka et al., xiii, xxii, 26, 58, 60

Brown, H. Rap, 97

Brown, Oscar C., Sr., 12, 55

Browne, Robert S., 20, 21, 60, 112, 118, 123

Bullock, Henry A., 74

Bunche, Ralph J., 5, 9

Bundy, McGeorge, 90

Burns, W. Haywood, 119

Burrell, Berkeley G., 116

Butcher, Margaret Just, 43

Cade, Toni, 43

Caldwell, Earl, 75

Caliguri, Joseph P., 61

Camp, Abraham, 4

Campbell, Laura, 72

Campbell, Robert, 4

Cardoso, Jack J., 75

Carmichael, Stokely, xx, xxi, 17, 21, 37, 44, 97, 102, 104

Carter, Lisle, 73

Carter, Robert L., 21

Cashin, John Logan, 108

Chamberlain, Gary L., 119

Chicago, University of, 76

Chisholm, Shirley, 44

Chrisman, Robert, 44

Ciochetto, Dante Peter, 44

Civil Rights Movement, xxiii

Civil War, 6, 96, 114

Clark, Kenneth B., ix, x, xiii,
     xxii, 21, 22, 39, 44, 45, 61,
     64, 73, 75, 76, 84, 86, 98, 119

Clark, Mamie Phipps, xiii

Clark, Peter L., 64

Clarke, John Henrik, 45, 46

Cleage, Albert B., Jr., 23, 37,
     38, 45, 119

Cleaver, Eldridge, 37, 52, 76, 98

Cleveland, Bernard, 76

Cleveland Convention (1854), 7

Cloward, Richard A., 34

Coalition of Black Trade Union-
     ists, 115

Cobbs, Price, 61, 72

Cochran, J. Otis, 72

Cohen, Robert Carl, 23

Coker, Daniel, 4

Cole, Johnnetta B., 45

Coles, Flournoy, 76

Columbia University, xiii, 72

Communism, 14, 104

Communist Party, 101, 103, 104

Community Action Agency, 105

Community Self-Determination
     Bill, 104, 116

Community Self-Development
     Act, 113

Conference of Black Political
     Scientists, 100

Conference of Negro Writers, 46

Conference on Black Power (1967).
     See National Conference on
     Black Power

Congress of Racial Equality
     (CORE), 3, 23, 30, 35, 37,
     39, 72, 102, 104, 113

Congressional Black Caucus, 95

Conyers, John, 108

Cooke, Anne. See Reid, Anne
     Cooke

Coombs, Orde, 46

CORE. See Congress of Racial
     Equality

Cornell University, xiii, 78; see
     also African Studies and
     Research Center

Cotton States and International
     Exposition (1895), 15

Craighead, William, 15

Crisis, 16

Cronon, Edmund David, 9, 38

Crowl, John A., 77

Crummell, Alexander, ix, 15

Cruse, Harold, xxiii, 23, 90

Cudjoe, Selwyn, 77

Cuffee, Paul, ix, 4, 5, 7

Cummings, Gwenna, 46

Cunningham, James, 46

Daniels, Deborah K., 62

Davis, Angela, 4

Davis, Arthur P., 46

Day, Noel A., 62

DeBarry, Clyde E., 23

Delany, Martin R., ix, 3, 4, 5, 7

Democratic National Convention
(1972), 95

Democratic Party, 97

Dent, Albert W., 94

Detroit, Mich., ix, 30, 64, 119

Dick, Robert C., 4

Dickinson, James C., 77

Dillard, J. L., 47

Dillon, Merton L., 77

Divine, Father, 28, 124

Doar, John, 64

Dodge Revolutionary Union Movement (DRUM), 111

Dodson, Dan, 27

Douglass, Frederick, 9, 10, 52

Dover, Cedric, 47

Dowey, Edward A., 120

Drake, St. Clair, xiii, 24

Draper, Theodore, 4

Dred Scott Decision, 3

DRUM. See Dodge Revolutionary
Union Movement

DuBois, W. E. B., xxi, xxiii,
5, 9, 10, 11, 16, 37, 43, 47,
62, 78, 85, 112, 120

Dunbar, Ernest, 78

Duncan, Joseph C., 72

Durley, Gerald L., 78

Dymally, Mervyn M., 108

East Palo Alto, Calif., 69

Edley, Christopher, 73

Educational Monument Association, 10

Edwards, Harry, 78

Ellison, Ralph, xiii, xv, xvi,
xviii, 24, 52

Engel, Robert, 78

Epps, Archie, 4

Erikson, Eric, 73

Essien-Udom, E. U., 24, 48

Etherington, Edwin D., 74

Fairfax, Ferdinando, 15

Faison, Adrienne, x

Farmer, James, 30, 32

Fashing, Joseph, 23

Feagin, Joe R., 24

Federation for Independent Political Action, 96

Fenderson, Lewis H., 40

Ferguson, Clyde, 73

Ferry, William H., 25, 98

Fichter, Joseph H., 120

Fisher, Miles M., 79

Fisher, Robert A., 79

Foner, Philip S., 98

Forman, James, 121, 123, 124, 126

Foster, Craig C., 89

Fourteenth Amendment, 60

Franklin, Benjamin, 33

Franklin, John Hope, xiii, 25, 65

Frantz, Thomas T., 79

Fraser, C. Gerald, 121

Frazier, E. Franklin, 5, 11, 48, 85, 121

Freedom Now Party, 108

Freeman, Linton C., 99

Frelow, Robert D., 62

Fugitive Slave Law, 3

Funnye, Clarence, 27

Furniss, W. Todd, 79

Gaffney, Floyd, 48

Galamison, Milton A., 25, 63, 68

Gallagher, Buell C., 79

Garland X, 48

Garnet, Henry Highland, ix, 3, 7

Garrison, William Lloyd, 5

Garvey, Marcus, ix, 3, 9, 11, 16, 38, 125

Garveyism, 13, 28, 38, 104, 120

Geis, Gilbert, 8

Genovese, Eugene D., 80

Georgia, 32

Gershman, Carl, 25

Gibson, Kenneth A., 108

Gifford, Bernard, xiii

Giles, Raymond H., Jr., 63

Ginsberg, Eli, 73

Gittell, Marilyn, 64

Glasgow, Douglas, 99

Gloster, Hugh M., 94

Godkin Lectures, 107

Goheen, Robert, 76

Goldman, Peter, 25, 46

Goldman, Samuel, 64

Gould, Geoffrey, 99

Grant, William R., 64

Great Society, The, 110

Grimke, Francis J., 11

Guardian, The, 15

Guinier, Ewart, 80, 85

Gulliver, Adelaide Cromwell, xiii, xv, xviii, 5, 27, 49

Hahn, Harlan, 99

Haley, Alex, 34

Hallman, Ralph J., 80

Hamilton, Charles V., 26, 37, 64, 81, 97, 99

Hampton, Fred, 98

Handlin, Oscar, 26

Harding, Vincent, 5, 26, 73, 81, 121

Hare, Nathan, 48, 49, 64, 72, 73, 81, 90

Harlem, 13, 64, 98

Harlem Board of Education Organizing Committee, 64

Harper, Frederick D., 82

Harrington, Donald Szantho, 121

Harris, Abram L., 116

Harris, Calvin, 23

Harris, Sheldon H., 5

Harris, William H., 49

Harrison, H., 65

Harvard University, xiii, 15, 56, 80, 82, 85, 107; see also Afro-American Studies Dept., W. E. B. DuBois Institute for Afro-American Research

Haskins, Kenneth W., 65

Hastie Group, xi, x, xv

Hastie, William H., xiii, xv, xix, 40, 49

Hatch, John, 83

Hatcher, Richard G., 100

Haverford College, ix, xiii, xv, xvi, xviii, xix

Hayes, President Rutherford B., 96

Henderson, George, 65

Henderson, Lenneal, 100

Henderson, Stephen E., 73

Henderson, Vivian W., 26

Henshel, Ann-Marie, 83

Henshel, Richard R., 83

Hentoff, Nat, 100

Higgins, Chester, 12

Hill, Adelaide Cromwell. See Gulliver, Adelaide Cromwell

Hill, Mozell C., 12

Hill, Norman, 86, 113

Hilliard, David, 98

Hobson, Julius, 112

Holman, M. Carl, xiii

Hopkins, Jeannette, x

Hopkins, Samuel, 15

Hopps, June G., 112

Hough, Joseph C., 122

Howard, John R., 27

Howe, Harold, 73

Howlett, Duncan, 122

Hudson, Herman, 83

Hughes, Langston, 46

Hunt, Deryl G., 100

Hunter, Charlayne, 27

Innis, Roy, 3, 27, 34, 104, 113

Interreligious Foundation for Community Organization, 12

Isaacs, Harold R., 28

Ivie, Stanley D., 83

Jack, Homer A., 119, 122

Jackson, Jesse L., 24, 113, 114, 115

Jackson, Maurice, 83

Jacobson, Julius, 114

Jacobson, Lenore, 67

Jencks, Christopher, 66, 84, 94

Jefferson, Thomas, 15

Jewish Theological Seminary, 121

Johnson, Clayton, 84

Johnson, Guy B., 12

Johnson, James Weldon, 12, 43

Johnson, Thomas A., 84

Jones, James M., 100

Jones, LeRoi. See Baraka, Amiri

Jones, Mack H., 101

Jones, Miles J., 122

Jordan, June, 49, 50, 84

Jordan, Vernon E., 28

Kansas, 13, 14

Kansas-Nebraska Act, 3

Karenga, Maulana Ron, 18, 46, 90

Keil, Charles, 50

Kerner Commission. See National Advisory Commission on Civil Disorders

Killens, John O., 50, 101, 114

Kilson, Martin, 5, 80, 84, 85, 90

King, Helen, 50

King, Martin Luther, Jr., 17, 24, 28, 87, 102, 107, 118, 120

Kirschenmann, Frederick, 29

Koontz, Elizabeth, 29

Kraft, Ivor, 66

Krosney, Herbert, 123

Labov, William, 51

Ladner, Joyce A., 29, 51

Langford, Anna R., 108

LaRue, Linda, 51

Lasch, Christopher, 101

League of Revolutionary Black Workers, 111

Lecky, Robert S., 123

Lee, Canada, 5

Leeds, Olly, 29

Lerner, Abba, 86

Lester, Julius, 29

Levi, Edward H., 76

Levine, Daniel U., 66

Levy, Joan D., 94

Lewis, Claude, 101

Lewis, Hylan, x, xiii, xv, xx, 51

Liberation Party, 106

Lightfoot, Claude, 101

Lincoln, Abraham, 8, 10

Lincoln, C. Eric, 30, 51, 123

Link, William R., 66

Llorens, David, 30

Locke, Alain, 43, 47

Lomax, Louis, 102, 123

Longino, Charles F., 52

Louisiana, 13, 32, 60

Luber, David, 121

Lynch, Hollis R., 6, 21

Lynn, Conrad, 27

Lythcott, Stephen, 86

McCabe, Edward P., 15, 36

McClintock, Ernie, 52

McConnell, Frank D., 52

Mack, Raymond W., 30

Mackey, James, 86

McKissick, Floyd B., 30, 99, 102, 105

McLauren, Dunbar S., 114

McLemore, Leslie Burl, 102

McPherson, James M., 6

McWorter, Gerald, 73

Malcolm X, 3, 17, 20, 25, 26, 30, 31, 32, 33, 34, 37, 39, 46, 52, 53, 56, 65, 126

Malcolm X Society, 19

March on Washington, 14, 102

Margolies, Edward, 52

Margolis, Richard J., 86

Marshall, Calvin B., 123

Marshall, Kenneth E., 114

Marshall, Ray, 115

Marx, Gary T., 123

Massey Lectures, 28

Matthew, Thomas W., 102

Mayhew, Lewis B., 86

Maynard, Robert C., 67

Mays, Benjamin, 94

Mboya, Tom, 31

Meier, August, 4

Menard, Orville D., 31

Merton, Robert K., 31

Messenger, 16, 109

Methodist Episcopal Church. See African Methodist Episcopal Church

Metropolitan Applied Research Center, Inc., ix, x, xiii

Meyers, Michael, 87

Mexico, 14

Michigan, University of, 93

Mills, Olive, 87

Mississippi, xx, 32, 102

Mississippi Freedom Democratic Party, 102

Monsky, Mark, 34

Moore, Richard B., 13

Morrison, Toni, 53

Morsell, John A., 31, 124

Muhammad, Elijah, 120, 124, 125, 126

Muse, Benjamin, 102

NAACP. See National Association for the Advancement of Colored People

Nairobi College, 69

Nairobi Day Schools, 69

Nation of Islam, 3, 48; see also Black Muslims

National Advisory Commission on Civil Disorders, 32

National Association for the Advancement of Colored People, 23, 35, 39, 49, 59, 67, 96, 104, 112, 124, 126

National Association of Afro-American Education, 71

National Black Economic Conference, 121

National Black Labor Congress, 114

National Black Power Congress, 121

National Black Women's Political Leadership Caucus Convention, 48

National Committee of Negro Churchmen, 124, 127

National Conference of Black Political Scientists, 101

National Conference on Black Power (1967), 20, 49, 68, 105

National Council of Churches, 127

National Economic Growth and Reconstruction Organization, 102

National Emigration Convention, 4

National Movement for the Forty-Ninth State, 9

National Urban League, 39

Neal, Larry, 53

NEGRO. See National Economic Growth and Reconstruction Organization

New York City, 31, 64

New York City Board of Education, 63, 64

Newark, N. J. , ix, 59, 103, 105, 106

Newman, Richard, 32

Newman, Richard M. , x

Newton, Huey P. , 98, 103

Nichols, David C. , 87

Nixon, Richard, 96

Nolan, William A. , 103

North Carolina, 99

Oakland, Calif. , 68

Obadele, Imari Abubakari, 32, 33

Obatala, J. K. , 13, 87

Oberlin College, viii

Ocean-Hill Brownsville, 63

O'Dell, John H. , 33

O. E. O. See Office of Economic Opportunity

Ofari, Earl, 115

Office of Economic Opportunity, 105

Ogilvie, Donald H. , 73, 89

Ohmann, Carol, 33

Oklahoma, 8, 12

Oklahoma Immigration Society, 15, 36

Oliver, E. D. , 88

O'Neil, Wayne, 93

Operation Breadbasket, 114, 115

Operation PUSH, 113

Ottley, Herb, 103

Owen, Chandler, 16, 109

Palmer, Edward N. , 13

Pan-Africanism, 5, 13, 18, 21, 68

Parenti, Michael, 33

Parker, Robert A. , 124

Parks, Paul, 64

Patterson, Orlando, 34

Payne, Daniel A. , 124

Peace Movement of Ethiopia, 9

Pease, Jane H. , 6

Pease, William H. , 6

Pennsylvania, University of, 93

Pentony, DeVere E. , 88

Pettigrew, Thomas F. , 34, 73

Pfautz, Harold W. , 67

Philadelphia, Pa. , 64

Pifer, Alan, 88

Pinkney, Alphonso, 103

Piven, Frances Fox, 27, 34

Plessy v. Ferguson, 13, 60

Poinsett, Alex, 104, 124

Poole, Elijah. See Muhammad, Elijah

Poor People's March. See March on Washington

Porter, Dorothy B. , 7

Porter, James A. , 53

Poussaint, Alvin F. , 24, 54, 90

Powell, Adam Clayton, Jr. , 35

President's Commission for the Observance of Human Rights, 73

President's Commission on Campus Unrest, 92

Princeton University, xiii

Proctor, Samuel, 88

Ranck, Lee, 125

Randolph, A. Philip, 5, 13, 14, 16, 109

Ras Tafarians, 52

Raspberry, William, 54

Reconstruction, 9

Record, Wilson, 35, 104

Redding, J. Saunders, xiii, xv, xxii, 14, 46, 54, 89

Redkey, Edwin S. , 14

Redmond, Eugene, 54

Reid, Anne Cooke, xiii, 46

Reid, Inez Smith, 89

Reimers, David M. , 125

Relyea, Harold C. , 125

Republic of New Africa, 4, 19, 30, 32, 37, 63, 79, 82, 86

Republican Party, 15, 97

Reynolds, Alfred W. , 14

Reynolds, L. H. , 126

Riesman, David, 84, 94

Rippy, J. Fred, 14

Rist, Ray C. , 89

Riverside Church, 121

R. N. A. See Republic of New Africa

Roberts, Gene, 104

Roberts, J. Deotis, 126

Roberts, Steven V. , 89

Robeson, Paul, 35

Robinson, Armstead L. , 89

Robinson, Isaiah E. , Jr. , 67

Roosevelt, Franklin D. , 73

Rosenthal, Robert, 67

Roucek, Joseph S. , 104

Rucker, Richard, 39

Rudwick, Elliot, 4

Russell, Carlos, 68

Russell, Michele, 68

Rustin, Bayard, 21, 35, 36, 85, 90, 105

Safa, Helen Icken, 55

Salaam, Kalamu, 105

Samuels, Gertrude, 126

San Francisco State College, 81

Satterwhite, Frank J. , 68

SCLC. See Southern Christian Leadership Conference

Schlesinger, Stephen C. , 115

Shockley, Ann Allen, 55

Schrag, Peter, 36

Schuchter, Arnold, 126

Schwartz, Robert, 68

Schwedmann, Glen, 14

Scottsboro Case, 104

Seale, Bobby, 98

Seder, John, 116

Sherrill, Robert, 36

Sherwood, Henry Noble, 7, 15

Shrine of the Black Madonna, 119

Sierra Leone, ix

Simmons, Kenneth, 27

Simpkins, Edward, 90

Sinnette, Calvin H., 36

Sizemore, Barbara A., 68

Skolnick, Jerome H., 55

Slater, Jack, 69

Sleeper, Charles Freeman, 127

Small Business Administration,
   115

Smith, Bob, 36

Smith, Edward C., 105

Smith, Holly, 55

Smith, Paul M., 69

Smith, William L., 72

Smitherman, Geneva, 56

SNCC. See Student Nonviolent
   Coordinating Committee

Socialism, 18, 115

Socialist Workers Party, 97

Sojourner, W.A., 88

Solomon, Victor, 27

Soul City, 99, 105

South Carolina, 32

Southern Christian Leadership
   Conference, 26, 28, 35, 39,
   102

Soviet Union, 35

Sowell, Thomas, 86, 90, 91

Spaights, Ernest, 91

Spero, Sterling D., 116

Spirit House, 106

Stember, Charles Herbert, 69

Stimpson, Catherine R., 69

Stone, Chuck, 105, 106

Storing, Herbert J., 36

Strickland, Dorothy S., 56

Stringfellow, William, 123

Strong, Mary, x

Stuckey, Sterling, 7

Student Nonviolent Coordinating
   Committee, 26, 35, 39, 72,
   97, 102

Sturdivant, Frederick D., 116

Sundiata, I. K., 91

Sunshine, Morris H., 99

Sutton, Percy, 108

Swarthmore College, xiii

Syracuse University. See All-
   University Summer Conference

Taylor, Orlando L., 91

Tax, Sol, 68

Terrell, Henry S., 111

Texas, 12

Texas, University of, 116

Thelwell, Mike, 92

Third World, 18

Thomas, Tony, 37

Thorne, Richard, 57

Tinker, Irene, 37

Toliver-Weddington, Gloria, 57

Tolson, Arthur, 15

Trotter, William Monroe, 15

Tucker, Sterling, 37

Turner, Darwin, 73

Turner, Henry M., 5, 57

Turner, James, 38, 92, 106

Tyler, Lawrence L., 116

Tyler, Robert, 57

U. F. T. See United Federation of
    Teachers

U. N. I. A. See Universal Negro
    Improvement Association

Unitarian Universalist Association,
    119, 122

United Church of Christ, 72

United Federation of Teachers, 63

United Methodist Church, 72

United Methodist National Convo-
    cation on the Black Church,
    125

United Presbyterian Church, 127

U. S. Commission on Civil Rights,
    69

U. S. House of Representatives,
    101

U. S. Senate Select Committee on
    Equal Educational Opportun-
    ity, 45

U. S. Supreme Court, xxii, 13

Universal Negro Improvement
    Association, ix, 9, 11, 38

Urban Research Corporation, 92

Vedlitz, Arnold, 60

Vincent, Theodore G., 38

Virginia Union University, 74

Vivian, C. T., 38

Vontress, Clemont E., 92

Wagoner, Jennings L., 52

Wahle, Kathleen O., 15

Walker, E. P., 3

Walters, Hubert, 57

Walters, Ronald, 64

Walton, Hanes, Jr., 106, 107

Walton, Sidney F., 72, 117

Ward, Francis, 57

Ward, Hiley H., 38

Ward, Val Gray, 57

Warren, Robert Penn, 39

Washington, Booker T., 9, 10, 15, 16, 38, 98

Washington, D.C., 64, 65

Watson, Bernard C., xiii, xv, xxii

Watts, Calif., ix, 32, 98

Weaver, Robert C., xiii, xv, xxiv, 107

W.E.B. DuBois Institute for Afro-American Research, Harvard University, 82

Weidlein, Edward R., 92

Weinstein, James, 16

Weisbord, Robert G., 7

Weiss, Samuel A., 39

Wesley, Charles, 8

Wesleyan University, 86; see also Afro-American Society

Whipper, William, 7, 8

White, Walter, 16, 43

Whiting, Albert N., 93

Wicker, Tom, 70

Wiesner, Jerome, 73

Wilcox, Preston R., 27, 64, 70, 93

Wilkins, Roy, 37, 39, 72, 86, 93

Wilkinson, Doreen H., 70

Willett, Lynn H., 78

Williams, Eddie N., xiii

Williams, Franklin H., xiii, 40

Williams, Maxine, 58

Williams, Robert Franklin, 19, 23

Willie, Charles V., 94

Wilmore, Gayraud S., 127

Wilson, James A., 39

Wilson, James Q., 108

Wilson, W.J., 10

Wolfe, Deborah Partridge, 121

Women of African Heritage, 52

Woodmansee, John J., 39

Woodson, Carter G., 16

Woodward, C. Vann, 39, 73, 86

World War I, ix, xx, 7, 16

World War II, 48, 122

Wormley, Stanton L., 40

Worthy, William, 108

Wright, H. Elliot, 123

Wright, James Skelley, 59

Wright, Major, 21

Wright, Nathan, 40, 108, 127

Wright, Richard, 42, 52, 58

Wright, Robert E., 117

Wright, Steven J., 94

Yale University, xiii; see also
    Black Student Alliance

Young, Whitney M., Jr., 37, 40,
    71

title index

A. Philip Randolph: A Biographical Portrait, 109

"Abolitionist and Negro Opposition to Colonization During the Civil War," 6

"Affinity of Negro Pupils for Segregated Schools: Obstacle to Desegregation, The," 60

"Africa Conscious Harlem," 13

"Aims and Objects of Movement for Solution of Negro Problems," 11

"A. L. A. Black Caucus Program Action Committee Proposal," 95

"Alabama Negro Colony in Mexico: 1894-96, The," 14

"Alexander Crummell: Black Evangelist," 15

"All Black Party, An," 108

"All-Negro Communities of Oklahoma: The Natural History of a Social Movement, The," 12

American Negro Art, 47

"American Negro Cannot Look to Africa for an Escape, The," 31

"American Negro College, The," 84

"American Negro College, Four Responses, The," 94

American Negro Revolution: From Nonviolence to Black Power, 1963-1967, The, 102

American Negro Writer and His Roots: Selected Papers, The, 46

"American Racial Crisis, The," 32

"American Racial Ideologies and Organizations in Transition," 35

"American Religion and the Negro," 120

American Revolution, The, 96

"America's Black Supremacists," 123

"America's Emerging Nation," 31

"Anatomy of the Black Studies Movement," 85

"Apartheid in American Higher Education," 93

"Applying Black Power: A Speculative Essay," 100

Apropos of Africa: Sentiments of Negro-American Leaders on Africa from the 1800s to the 1950s, 5

"Are Black Studies Relevant?" 83

"Artist and the Black University, The," 101

"Artist in the Black University, The," 50

"Assimilation and Counter-Assimilation: From Civil Rights to Black Radicalism," 33

"Assimilation of Afro-Americans, The," 103

Autobiography of Malcolm X, The, 52, 65

"Autobiography of Malcolm X, The: A Revolutionary Use of the Franklin Tradition," 33

"Back-to-Africa Idea, The," 7

"Battle for Black Studies, The," 81

"Berkeley Plan for Desegregation, The," 62

Beyond Racism: Building an Open Society, 40

"Birth of a (Black) Nation," 19

"Black Activists and the Schools," 19

"Black Activists for Liberation, Not Guidance," 69

"Black American Epic: Its Roots, Its Writers," 54

"Black Artist—His Role in the Struggle," 57

"Black Arts Movement in Negro Poetry, The," 54

Black Awakening in Capitalist America: An Analytic History, 3

Black Capitalism in Economic Perspective, 110

"Black Capitalism: Toward Controlled Development of Black America," 117

"Black Caucus: A Meaningful Course of Action, The," 95

"Black Caucus in Congress, The," 101

"Black Caucus in the Unions," 115

"Black Church—Its Mission Is Liberation, The," 123

"Black College and the New Black Awareness, The," 74

"Black Colleges: Vital Part of American Education," 72

"Black Colonies: A Modest Proposal," 25

"Black Community, the Community School, and the Specialization Process: Some Caveats, The," 67

"Black Control: In Search of Humanism," 70

Black Crusader: A Biography of Robert Franklin Williams, 23

"Black Culture/White Teacher," 69

"Black Economic Liberation Under Capitalism," 109

Black Education: Myths and Tragedies, 90

"Black Elected Officials in the South," 96

Black English: Its History and Usage in the United States, 47

"Black English: Route or Roadblock to Racial Progress?" 42

"Black English: The Politics of Translation," 49

Black Exodus, Black Nationalism and Back-to-Africa Movements, 1890-1910, 14

"Black Higher Education and Its Challenges," 74

"Black Intellectuals Divided over Ideological Directions," 27

"Black Is Beautiful vs. White Is Right," 56

Black Jews of Harlem, The, 118

"Black Labor and the Black Liberation Movement," 114

"Black Leaders Speak Out on Black Education," 72

Black Liberation and Socialism, 37

Black Manifesto: Religion, Racism and Reparations, 123

"'Black Manifesto': Revolution, Reparation, Separation, The," 120

"Black Man's View of Authority, A," 23

"Black Messiah, The," 119

Black Moses, 9

"Black Movement and Women's Liberation, The," 51

"Black Music and the Black University," 57

Black Muslims in America, The, 123

"Black Muslims in America: A Reinterpretation," 119

"Black Mystique Pitfall, The," 49

"Black Nationalism," 3

"Black Nationalism and Community Schools," 67

"Black Nationalism and the Schools," 65

Black Nationalism in America, 4

"Black Nationalism: The Early Debate," 16

"Black Nationalism: The Inevitable Response," 38

Black Nationalism: The Search for an Identity in America, 48

"Black Nationalists' Plan for Splitting of 5 States," 19

"Black Neo-Segregationists, The," 19

"Black Nonsense," 42

Black Panther, The, 98

Black Panthers Speak, The, 98

Black Perspective on Community Control, A," 65

Black Political Parties—An Historical and Political Analysis, 106

Black Political Power in America, 105

Black Politics—A Theoretical and Structural Analysis, 106

"Black Power," 124

"Black Power—An Advocate Defines It," 45

"Black Power and Black Population: A Dilemma," 23

"Black Power and Black Students in Kansas City," 61

Black Power and Christian Responsibility: Some Biblical Foundations for Social Ethics, 127

"Black Power and the American Christ," 121

Black Power and the American Myth, 38

Black Power and the Garvey Movement, 38

Black Power and Urban Unrest: Creative Possibilities, 127

Black Power and White Protestants: A Christian Response to the New Negro Pluralism, 122

"Black Power Confronts Unitarian Universalists," 122

"Black Power: Cultural Nationalism as Politics," 101

"Black Power: Implications for the Urban Educator," 66

"Black Power in Christological Perspective," 118

"Black Power on the Campus: Implications for Admissions Officers and Registrars," 88

"Black Power: Right or Left?" 112

"Black Power—The Debate in 1840," 6

Black Power: The Politics of Liberation in America, 97

"Black Power Through Community Control," 99

"Black Pride? Some Contradictions," 46

"Black Radicalism: The Road from Montgomery," 26

"Black Revolt Hits the White Campus, The," 78

"Black Revolt in White Churches," 124

"Black Revolution and Education, The," 61

"Black Revolution and the Economic Future of Negroes in the United States, The," 74

"Black Revolution in American Studies, The," 89

"Black Self-Determination: A Debate," 113

"Black Separatism," 18, 55

"Black Separatism in Perspective: Movement Reflects Failure of Integration," 30

"Black Separatism: Shock of Integration," 25

"Black Separatists: Attitudes and Objectives in a Riot-torn Ghetto," 99

Black Seventies, The, 96

"Black Staff, Black Studies, and White Universities: A Study in Contradictions," 89

"Black Strategies for Change in America," 37

"Black Students and the Impossible Revolution," 81

"Black Students Revolt on the White Campus," 82

"Black Studies: A Cop-Out?" 91

"Black Studies: A Political Perspective," 92

"Black Studies Aim to Change Things," 89

"Black Studies: An American View," 72

"Black Studies: An Intellectual Crisis," 73

"Black Studies and Black Separatism," 73

"Black Studies and Higher Education," 76

"Black Studies and Sound Scholarship," 94

"Black Studies at Antioch," 86

"Black Studies—Boon or Bane?" 92

"Black Studies: Bringing Back the Person," 84

"Black Studies: Can They Be Really Relevant?" 83

"Black Studies: Challenge to Higher Education," 92

"Black Studies: Here to Stay?" 90

"Black Studies in the College Curriculum," 76

Black Studies in the University, 89

"Black Studies Movement: A Plea for Perspective," 85

Black Studies, Myths and Realities, 85

"Black Studies Programs: An Analysis," 89

Black Studies Programs in Public Schools, 63

"Black Studies Programs: Issues and Problems," 91

"Black Studies Programs: Promises and Pitfalls," 83

"Black Studies Stop the Shouting and Go to Work," 87

"Black Studies: The Bitterness and Hostility Lessen, but Criticism Persists," 77

"Black Studies: The Real Issue," 83

"Black Studies: The Universities in Moral Crisis," 86

"Black Studies Thing, The," 78

"Black Studies: Trouble Ahead," 80

"Black Theatre: Commitment and Communication," 48

"Black Theological Education: Programming for Liberation," 126

"Black University: A Revolutionary Educational Concept Designed to Serve the Total Black Community, The," 73

Black Woman; An Anthology, The, 43

"Black Woman and Women's Lib, The," 50

"Black Women—Often Discussed but Never Understood," 46

"Black Women Turn from 'Feminism,'" 48

"Black Words and Black Becoming," 52

Black Worker: The Negro and the Labor Movement, The, 116

"Blacks and the Crisis of Political Participation," 99

"Blacks at Harvard: Crisis and Change," 85

"Blacktown and Whitetown: The Case for a New Federalism," 98

Blues People; Negro Music in White America, 42

"Booby Trap of Black Separatism, The," 21

Brotherhood of Sleeping Car Porters: Its Origin and Development, The, 110

Brown et al. v. Board of Education of Topeka et al., xiii, xxii, 26, 58, 60

By Any Means Necessary, 20

Campus and the Racial Crisis, The, 87

"Campus Racial Tensions Rise as Black Enrollment Increases," 84

"Can There Any Good Thing Come Out of Nazareth?" 35

"Case Against Blackthink, The," 36

"Case Against Separatism: 'Black Jim Crow,' The," 93

"Case for a New Black Church Style, The," 127

"Case for All-Black Schools, The," 62

"Case for an Independent Black Political Party, The," 97

"Case for Black Separatism, The," 20

"Case for Black Student Power, The," 77

"Case for Black Studies, The," 88

"Case for Independent Black Trade Unions, The," 110

"Case for Negro Separatism, The," 55

"Case for Separatism: Black Perspective, The," 81

"Case for Two Americas—One Black, One White, The," 20

"CBE Interviews: Kenneth B. Clark," 44

"Center for Black Students on University Campuses, A," 78

A Century of Negro Migration, 16

"Challenge of Black Student Organizations, The," 60

"Changing Aspiration, Images and Identities," 51

"Charade of Power: Black Students at White Colleges, A," 75

"City Is the Black Man's Land, The," 96

"Code of Ethics," 109

College and the Black Student: NAACP Tract for the Times, 79

"College and the Urban Community: Racial Insularity and National Purpose, The," 88

"College Chiefs Urge Ethnic Centers," 75

"Colleges Are Skipping Over Competent Blacks to Admit 'Authentic' Ghetto Types," 90

"Colleges Scored on Segregation," 84

"Colored Men as Professors in Colored Institutions," 11

"Columbia and the New Left," 72

"Come to the Land," 32

"Coming of the Black Ghetto State, The," 105

Communism Versus the Negro, 103

"Community-Centered School, The," 70

"Community Control: Separatism Repackaged," 105

"Community Control vs. School Integration—the Case of Detroit," 64

Community Schools: Education for Change, 70

"Complete Integration Must Be the Goal," 29

"Confronting Monopoly and Keeping the Movement Moving," 113

"Consciousness of Negro Nationality to 1900," 3

"Contours of the 'Black Revolution' in the 1970s, The," 33

Crisis of the Negro Intellectual, The, 23

"Crisis Which Bred Black Power, The," 40

"Critical Analysis of the Tactics and Programs of Minority Groups, A," 9

"Culture: Negro, Black and Nigger," 45

Cutting Edge: Social Movements and Social Change in America, The, 27

"Danger and Necessity of Black Separatism, The," 29

"Danger of White Liberalism, The," 70

"Dangerous Inefficiency of Racially Separated Schools, The," 61

Death and Life of Malcolm X, The, 25, 46

Death of White Sociology, The, 29

"Decentralization Revisited," 64

"Demands of Black Students: A Mixed Bag," 79

"Dialogue on Separatism, A," 24

Die Nigger Die!, 97

"Dilemma of the Afro-American, The," 27

Dilemmas of Urban America, 107

"Does the Negro Need Separate Schools?" 62

Down the Line, the Collected Writings of Bayard Rustin, 35

Dusk of Dawn: An Essay Toward an Autobiography of a Race Concept, 10

"Early Negro Deportation Projects," 15

Early Negro Writing 1760-1837, 7

"East River, Downtown: Postscript to a Letter from Harlem," 17

"Economic Case for Reparations to Black America," 112

"Economic Developments in the Black Community," 110

"Economic Integration and the Progress of the Negro Community," 110

"Economic Potential of Black Capitalism, The," 111

"Education and Revolution," 76

Education by, for and about African Americans: A Profile of Several Black Community Schools, 62

"Education for Black Liberation," 70

Education of Black Folk; the Afro-American Struggle for Knowledge in White America, The, 71

"Educational Criticism and the Transformation of Black Consciousness," 52

"Educational Decision-Making," 60

"Educational Implications of Black Studies," 78

"Eleven Days at Brandeis—As Seen from the President's Chair, The," 71

"Elijah Muhammad," 120

"Engineers of Black Liberation," 100

"Erased, Debased, and Encased: The Dynamics of African Educational Colonization in America," 68

"Ethos of the Blues, The," 53

"Evaluating Effects of the Integrated Classroom," 69

"Exodus: Black Zionism," 13

"Expression of Negro Militancy in the North, 1840-1860," 3

"Extended Memorandum on the Programs, Ideologies, Tactics, and Achievements of Negro Betterment and Interracial Organizations," 9

"Extremist Movements Among American Negroes," 35

"Extremists and the Schools: A Context for Understanding," 65

"Failure of Black Separatism, The," 36

"Failure: Three Experts Discuss It, and What Could Be Done, The," 45

"Fake Panaceas for Ghetto Education," 68

"Fantasy of Black Nationalism, The," 4

"Farewell to Integration," 98

"Feud Within the Black Muslims," 126

Fire-Bell in the Night: The Crisis in Civil Rights, 26

First Three Years of the Afro-American Studies Department, 1969-1972, The, 82

"Floyd McKissick, Architect of Soul City, a Bold New Experiment in Living," 105

"Formation of a Revolutionary Black Culture," 44

"Fragmented Movement, The," 17

"Futility of Black Self-Segregation," 31

Future of the American Negro, The, 16

"Geographic Proposals for Black Economic Liberation," 117

Getting It Together: Black Businessmen in America, 116

"Ghetto and Gown: The Birth of Black Studies," 79

"Ghetto Blacks and College Policy," 75

"Ghetto Economic Development," 114

"Gnawing Dilemma: Separatism and Integration, 1865-1925, The," 9

"God Is a Negro," 57

"Grammar and Goodness," 56

"Group of Intellectuals Were Fed Up with Maltreatment," 12

"Has 'Benign Neglect' Invaded the Churches?" 119

Here I Stand, 35

Higher Education of Blacks in the United States, The, 88

History of the African Methodist Episcopal Church, 124

"Housing Policy for Metropolitan Areas," 107

"How Negroes Rediscovered Their Racial Pride," 51

"How White Power Whitewashes Black Power," 48

"Human, All Too Human: The Negro's Vested Interest in Segregation," 11

""I Want to Use Your Blackness,'" 125

Ideological Origins of Black Nationalism, The, 7

"Importance of Black Colleges, The," 84

"Incredible Messiah; The Deification of Father Divine, The," 124

"Insiders and Outsiders: A Chapter in the Sociology of Knowledge," 31

"Integrated or Separate: Which Road to Progress?" 27

"Integration," 39

Integration and Separation in Education, 64

"Integration and the Negro Mood," 28

"Integration Must Work—Nothing Else Can, " 25

"Integration or Black Nationalism: Which Route Will Negroes Choose?" 57

"Interview with John Hope Franklin, " 65

"Is There a Case for Separate Schools?" 68

"Jesse Jackson and Operation Breadbasket: In Search of a New Alternative, " 114

"Jim Crow, " 10

Kawaida Studies: The New Nationalism, 18

Language in the Inner City: Studies in the Black English Vernacular, 51

"Learning Is an All-Black Thing, " 69

"Letter from Birmingham Jail, " 28

"Letter of Resignation from Board of Directors of Antioch College, " 75

"Letter to Americans, A, " 17

"Letter to Black Educators in Higher Education, A, " 93

Letter to Edward H. Levi, 76

Letter to Homer A. Jack, 119

Letter to Robert Goheen, 76

"Letter to W. J. Wilson, August 8, 1865, " 10

"Liberation, " 19

"Limits of Black Capitalism, The, " 116

"Lincoln's Plan for Colonizing the Emancipated Negroes, " 8

"Literature of the Negro in the United States, The, " 58

Longest Way Home: Chief Alfred C. Sam's Back-to-Africa Movement, The, 8

"Making of Black Revolutionaries, The, " 121

"Malcolm X: Mission and Meaning, " 39

Many Shades of Black, 40

"Many Thousands Gone, " 42

"Media for Change: Black Students in the White University, " 82

Message to the Black Man in America, 125

"Militant Separatists in the White Academy, The, " 49

"Minorities and Community Control of the Schools, " 71

"Minority Enterprise—The Need for Bold Initiatives and Staunch Allies," 111

"Mississippi Freedom Democratic Party," 102

Modern Negro Art, 53

"More Blacks, but Less Integration: Black Youth, Black Nationalism and White Independent Schools," 66

Muhammad Speaks, 120

"Musical Culture of Afro-America, The," 57

My Face Is Black, 30

Myth of Black Capitalism, The, 115

"NAACP and 'Reparations,' The," 124

"NAACP: Faith and an Opportunity," 59

"NAACP Suspends Atlanta Unit; Repudiates School Agreement," 67

"Nation Time or Integration Time?" 103

"National Association for Equal Opportunity in Higher Education: Crusader for the Black College," 79

"National Conference on Black Power, The," 105

"Nationalism in a Plural Society: The Case of the American Negro," 37

"Nationalist Movements of Harlem, The," 24

"Nationalist vs. the Integrationist, The," 26

Native Sons: A Critical Study of Twentieth Century Negro American Authors, 52

"Necessity for Separation, The," 29

"Need for a Cultural Base to Civil Rites and Bpower Mooments, The," 18

"Needed: A Black Studies Consortium," 77

"Negro American: His Self-Image and Integration, The," 54

Negro Americans, What Now? 12

"Negro and American Values, A Conversation Between James Farmer and Algernon D. Black, The," 32

Negro and Organized Labor, The, 115

Negro and the American Labor Movement, The, 114

"Negro and the Urban Crisis, The," 22

Negro Church in America, The, 121

"Negro College, The," 78

"Negro Colonization in the Reconstruction Era, 1865-1870,"
8

"Negro Colonization Project in
Mexico, 1895, A," 14

"Negro Convention Movement, The,"
6

"Negro Elected Public Official in
the Changing American Scene,
The," 98

Negro Genius, The, 43

Negro in American Culture, The,
43

"Negro in American Politics,
The," 100

"Negro in Politics, The," 108

Negro in the United States, The,
48

Negro in Third Party Politics,
The, 107

"Negro Nationalism a Black Power Key," 104

Negro Novel in America, The, 43

"Negro Opposition to Black Extremism, The," 30

"Negro Secret Societies," 13

"Negro Separatism in the Colleges," 85

"Negro Separatist Movement of the
Nineteenth Century, A," 4

"Negro Woman in Retrospect: A
Blueprint for the Future, The,"
55

"Negroes in an Integrated Society,"
111

"Neighboring Black and White
Colleges: A Study in Waste,"
86

"New Afro-American Nationalism,
The," 45

"New Black Myths, The," 36

"New Civil Rights Struggle, The,"
28

"New Directions for American
Education: A Black Perspective," 91

"New Meaning for 'Black Power',"
102

New Negro, The, 47

New Perspectives on Black Studies, 73

"Newark Teachers' Strike, The,"
59

"No More Nonsense About Ghetto
Education," 59, 68

No More Strangers, 118

No Name in the Street, 17

"Note from a Black Political Scientist, A," 101

"Now Hear the Message of the
Black Muslims from Their
Leader, Elijah Muhammad,"
124

"Now It's a Negro Drive for Segregation," 32

"Ocean Hill-Brownsville Dispute: Urban School Crisis in Microcosm," 63

"Oklahoma's All-Black State Movement, 1889-1907," 15

"On Being Ashamed of Oneself, an Essay on Race Pride," 47

On Being Negro in America, 14

On Race Relations, 11

"On the Black University," 93

"On White Campuses, Black Students Retreat into Separatism," 94

"Only Way to Redeem Africa, The," 13

"Opposition to Black Separatism," 8

"Ordeal of Malcolm X, The," 39

"Organized Negro Communities: A North American Experiment," 6

"Other Hill, The," 19

"Our Book Shelf," 47

"Our Goal Is Individual Freedom," 97

"Pan-Negro Nationalism in the New World, Before 1862," 6

Partisan Review, 42

Patterns of Residential Segregation, 99

"Paul Cuffee," 7

Paul Cuffee: Black America and the African Return, 5

"Penthouse Interview/Roy Innis, Black Nationalist," 34

"Perspective on Black Acting," 52

Planning an Independent Black Educational Institution, 68

"Planning Model for Black Community Development, A," 112

"Playboy Interview: Jesse Jackson," 115

"Playboy Interviews: Malcolm X," 34

Plessy v. Ferguson, 13, 60

"Plight of Black Students in the United States, The," 91

"Political Dimensions of Black Liberation, The," 100

Political Philosophy of Martin Luther King, Jr., The, 107

"Politics of Bidialectalism," 53

"Potential of Black Capitalism, The," 109

"Power and Racism: What We Want," 44

Prejudice and Your Child, 22

"Preparation for Life: The Black Classroom," 67

"Present and Future of the Colored Race in America, The," 10

Preuves, 24

"Private Schools for Black Children," 66

"Programs for Black Power," 102

Prophet of the Black Nation, 38

Prophetic Liberator of the Coloured Race of the United States of America: Command to His People, 8

Proposal for an Independent Harlem School System, 64

"Prospects for the Future," 24

"Protestant Ethic Among the Black Muslims, The," 116

"Public School Segregation in the Seventies," 61

Pygmalion in the Classroom, 67

"Question of Black Studies," 81

"Race and Education: A Search for Legitimacy," 64

Race and Radicalism: The NAACP and the Communist Party in Conflict, 104

"Race, Revolution and Women," 44

"Racial Diversity Unsettles Wesleyan," 74

Racial Isolation in the Public Schools, 69

"Racial Minorities and Curriculum Change," 79

"Racial Self-Fulfillment and the Rise of an All-Negro Community in Oklahoma," 8

Racially Separate or Together? 34

"Racism and Anti-Feminism," 44

"Racist Church? Black Clergy Conference," 125

Raise Race Rays Raze: Essays Since 1965, 18

"Rationale for Black Studies, A," 86

"Reflections on the Black Woman's role in the Community of Slaves," 4

"Religion and Resistance Among Ante-bellum Negroes, 1800-1861," 5

"Religion: Opiate or Inspiration of Civil Rights Militance Among Negroes?" 123

Reparations: Black Manifesto and Its Challenge to White America, 126

"Repatriation—Dead Issue or Res- urrected Alternative?" 36

Report of the Faculty Committee on African and Afro-American Studies, 82

"Republic of New Africa: The Struggle for Land in Mississip- pi," 32

"Rethinking Black History," 34

"Retreat to Separate but Equal," 66

"Retrospective View: Black Sep- aratism at Antioch, A," 87

"Return to the Campus, The," 78

"Rev. Milton A. Galamison: Man of Action," 68

"Revolt of Poor Black Women, The," 55

Revolution and Nation Building, 33

Revolutionary Suicide, 103

"Rhetoric of Ante-bellum Black Separatism," 4

"Right of Black America to Cre- ate a Black Nation, The," 101

"Rise of 'Black Power' in the United States, The," 104

"Role of the Black Lawyer in To- day's Black Revolution, The," 21

"Ron Karenga and Black Cultural Nationalism," 46

"Roy Innis: Nation-Builder," 104

"St. Louis and the 'Exodusters' of 1879," 14

"Scale of Black Separatism, A," 39

"Scope of Black English, The," 57

Search for a Place; Black Sep- aratism and Africa, 1860, 4

"Segregated Professional Asso- ciation?" 116

"Segregation," 112

"Segregation—a Symposium," 16

"Separate Is Not Equal," 90

"Separation," 20

"Separation or Integration: A Debate," 30

Separatism or Integration: Which Way for America? 21

"Separatism Path Urged for Blacks," 121

"Separatism? We Are Separated— and That's the Cause of All Our Woes," 40

"Separatist Economics: A New Social Contract," 113

"Separatists' Fantasy, The," 29

Shadow and Act, 24

"Short-range Separatism, " 114

"Should Ghettoese Be Accepted?"
54

"Sin, Separatism, Solidarity and
the Future of Race Relations, "
121

"Social Scientists, the Brown Decision, and Contemporary Confusion, The, " 45

"Sociology of Black Nationalism,
The, " 106

"Some Factors in the Development
of Negro Social Institutions in
the United States, " 12

"Soul City, " 99

Speech to the Third Annual Dinner
of the Congressional Black Caucus, 97

Speeches of Malcolm X at Harvard,
The, 56

"Standard or Nonstandard: Is
There an Answer?" 55

"Strategies and Tactics of an
Afro-American Party, " 95

"Strivings of the Negro People, "
11

Stokely Speaks: Black Power Back
to Pan-Africanism, 21

"Support Builds for RNA Eleven;
RNA Fact Sheet, " 37

"Talk Up Racism, " 37

"Tears for the Pigs, " 98

"Theology of Black Power, The, "
125

"They Think You're an Airplane
and You're Really a Bird!"
106

"Third Force, Third Party or
Third-Class Influence?" 106

Thoughts on African Colonization,
5

"Thoughts on Black Power, " 22

"Three Challenges to Organized
Labor, " 113

Three-Fifths of a Man, 30

"Three Writers on the Question
of Repatriation, " 21

Time of the Furnaces, The,
71

Time to Speak, A Time to Act:
The Movement in Politics, A,
96

Tomorrow's Tomorrow: The
Black Woman, 51

"Toward a Sociology of Black
Studies, " 83

"Toward Ideological Clarity, "
18

"Toward Making 'Black Power'
Real Power, " 118

"Toward the Creation of Political
Institutions for All African
Peoples, " 95

"Traditionally White Institutions:
For Most, Still a Long Way
to Go, The, " 92

"True Solution of the Negro Problem, The," 11

Trumpet of Conscience, The, 28

"Two Nations at Wesleyan University, The," 86

"Two Ways: Black Muslim and N.A.A.C.P.," 126

"Two Worlds of Race: A Historical View, The," 25

"Unitarian Universalist Response to the Black Rebellion, A," 122

Urban Blues, 50

"Viable Black Community, The," 100

"Viewpoint: The New Black Apartheid," 87

"Voluntary Segregation: One Viewpoint," 87

What Black Politicians Are Saying, 108

"What Black Studies Mean to a Black Scholar," 81

"What Chance for Black Power?" 34

What Country Have I? 36

"What Does Non-violence Mean? In the Face of War and Death," 18

"What Is Africa to Us?" 49

"When 'Nonviolence' Meets 'Black Power'," 102

"What the Black Woman Thinks About Women's Lib," 53

"What We Mean by the Black University," 71

"What's Happening to America?" 39

"What's in a Name? Negro vs. Afro-American vs. Black," 42

When the Word Is Given, 123

"Where Did Their Revolution Go?" 87

Where Do We Go From Here: Chaos or Community? 28

"Where It's At: Civil Rights," 22

"White English in Blackface Or, Who Do I Be?" 56

"White English: The Politics of Language," 50

"White Faces and Black Studies," 77

White Man, Listen!, 58

"White Paper on Black Studies," 80

"White Power and Black Supremacy," 39

White Protestantism and the Negro, 125

"White Separatists and Black Separatists: A Comparative Analysis, 24

"Whitey's Reaction to Proposal of
Separate Black State, " 36

"Why a Black Seminary?" 122

"Why Negro Churches Are a Necessity, " 126

"Why Should We March?" 14

"Why Women's Liberation Is Important to Black Women, " 58

"Will the Church Remove the
Color Line?" 120

"Workers, Black and White:
DRUMbeats in Detroit, " 111